Parties With
Pizzazz

This book is dedicated to our families.
We would like to thank them
for their encouragement, support, and love.

Acknowledgements:
Jody Ebert - Cover Photographer
Marijo Ose - Editorial Consultant
Lisa Kempston - Cover Design Consultant
Dylan Mohan, Hannah Mohan & Peyton Udo - Our Cover Stars
Al Tollefson, TSI Marketing, Advertising & Design - Production

Parties With Pizzazz
ISBN 0-9744936-0-0
© Copyright 2004 by Peggy Simenson, Marci Mohan & Jeanne Palmer
Pizzazz Publishing

Pizzazz Publishing
P.O. Box 415
Victoria, Minnesota 55386
(952) 368-1903
www.pizzazzpublishing.com

Published by Pizzazz Publishing
P.O. Box 415
Victoria, Minnesota 55386

Table of Contents

Valentine Games

Valentine Crafts

Valentine Treats

Reproducible Pages

Let's Party!!

These two simple words create anticipation and excitement in the minds of children, but can be overwhelming to the party planner. As classroom teachers and parents ourselves we too felt overwhelmed when we had to plan parties for our students. No one wants a ho-hum party with activities that have been used over and over again. So what's the alternative?

Parties with Pizzazz was created in response to parents and teachers who need guidance in developing creative party ideas. *Parties with Pizzazz* makes party planning exciting, interactive, and most of all easy.

Parties with Pizzazz is unique in that it plans a party from start to finish. The party begins by involving everyone in a group activity called a mixer. Then the students get involved in a team builder, which separates the children into small groups. Within these small groups, the students continue the party by creating crafts, playing games, and making treats.

Even though *Parties with Pizzazz* was intended for classroom use the activities can be adapted for non-classroom groups of children, birthday parties, neighborhood get-togethers, community events, church groups and more.

We know you will enjoy *Parties with Pizzazz*. Have fun creating memorable events with children.

Let's Party!

Marci Mohan
Jeanne Palmer
Peggy Simenson

How to Use this Book

Parties With Pizzazz gives the party planner everything needed to host a successful and memorable party from start to finish. Any or all of the five components can be selected to create a unique party experience.

Mixers: The kick off to the party is called a mixer. It involves the entire class and is a great way to introduce the party theme and build excitement for the party.

Team Builders: A team builder is a unique way to divide the class into smaller groups. The team builders are designed to form four groups of students. These groups will rotate through stations, which could include: games, crafts and snacks. While the students rotate from station to station, parent volunteers remain at one station for the duration of the party. To initiate the rotation, use a signal such as light flicking, bell ringing or whistling. The station activities should take approximately the same amount of time, preferably 10 – 15 minutes.

Games: Games can be played either at stations or can be played by bringing the entire group together.

Crafts: Crafts can be assembled in stations or as a whole class activity. It is important for the facilitator to prepare an example of each craft in advance of the party in order to assist the parent volunteer in demonstrating the steps to make the craft.

Treats: Treats are often the highlight of the party. Children can create, assemble and eat their treats either in a station or as a whole group conclusion to the party. Due to many school restrictions, all snack ideas included in this book are prepared with store-bought ingredients. It is very important to determine whether any of the children have food allergies before selecting the treat.

A typical party would look like this:

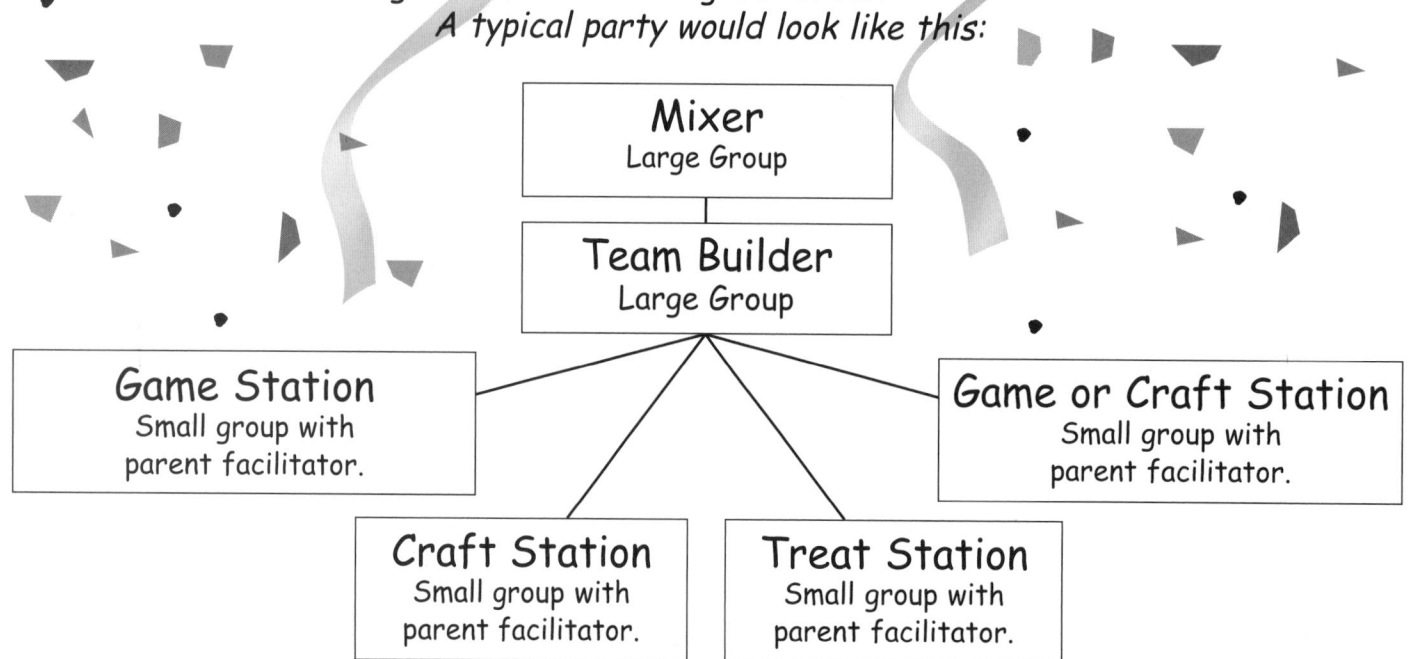

6

Party Planning Worksheet

Party Theme _____ Party Date _____ Time _____

Party Coordinator _____ Phone _____

Parent Volunteers   Phone Numbers

_____   _____

_____   _____

_____   _____

_____   _____

_____   _____

Party Events

	Activity	Parent Volunteer	Materials Needed
Mixer			
Team Builder			
Craft Station			
Game Station			
Treat Station			
Additional Station			

Halloween Mixers

A mixer is the kick-off activity to the party. It involves the entire class, building excitement for the party and setting the stage for fun.

A Web of Treats

You Need:
- craft sticks
- black yarn
- small prizes (pencils, candy, erasers)

Before the Party:
- For each student, cut a strand of black yarn long enough to weave around the classroom.
- Tie a prize at one end of the yarn.
- Wrap the yarn around the prize.
- Tie a craft stick to the other end of the yarn.

1. To prepare for this mixer students need to be out of the classroom for approximately 15 minutes.

2. Tape all the craft sticks to three or four desks that have been placed near the entrance to the classroom.

3. Unwind the yarn from each stick around the room, over and under desks and around chairs, to form a large web.

4. Before allowing the students to enter the room, tell them this tale:

"I just discovered that moments ago a tremendous tarantula crept down this hall and snuck into (teacher's name) room. This, however, was no ordinary spider. This was Tabitha the Tarantula, the great Halloween spider. She appears only once a year to spin her special web of treats. This year she selected your class to be the lucky students who see her unusual web. When you enter the classroom you are to take a craft stick and follow your way through the web by winding the yarn around the craft stick. At the end of the yarn you'll find a treat that Tabitha left for you."

5. As students enter one at a time, they choose any craft stick and begin winding up the yarn around their stick following a path through the web until they discover their prize.

Eyewitness Sketch

<u>You Need:</u>
- drawing paper
- crayons/markers
- pencils

1. Tell the students, *"A Halloween prank has been committed. It was reported that a bully has been stealing trick or treat goodie bags. Police were lucky to have _____ (name of adult who will read the description in step 4) as an eyewitness. Now the police need your help as a sketch artist in drawing a picture they could use to identify the prankster."*

2. Pass out drawing paper.

3. Have the students close their eyes and listen to the full description before they draw their sketch.

"The prankster was a tall boy with a curly red wig. He wore a black and gold football jersey with the number 12 on the front. Bright red lipstick outlined his mouth and on his feet he wore yellow boots. The bully wore extra large sunglasses and a polka-dot tie."

4. Give the students five minutes to sketch their picture then quickly share the drawings with the group. End by saying, *"No one here looks like the Halloween bully. What a relief! There are no pranksters in our room. Let the party begin!"*

<u>Before the Party:</u>
- Reproduce the word cards on page 115.

Opposites Attract

1. Give each player one word card.

2. Children form pairs by looking for the person holding the word card with the opposite meaning of the word on their own card.

3. When everyone has found their partner, form a circle and share all the words.

Hooky Spooky

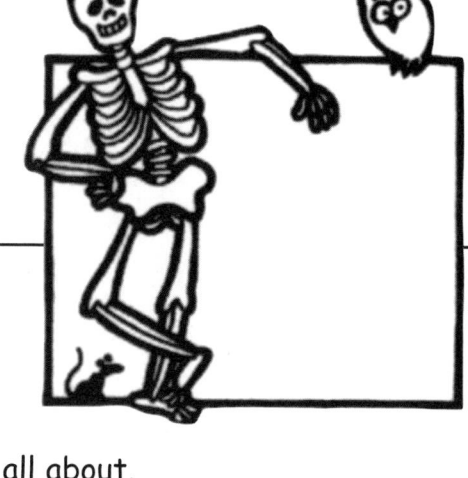

Gather the class in a large circle.
Sing the words below to the tune of the "Hokey Pokey."

Verse 1:   You put your hand bones in.
            You put your hand bones out.
            You put your hand bones in and you shake 'em all about.
            You do the hooky spooky and you rattle all around.
            That's what it's all about - BOO!

Chorus: You do the hooky spooky! You do the hooky spooky!
            You do the hooky spooky! That's what it's all about - BOO!

Verse 2:   foot bones

Verse 3:   skull bone

Verse 4:   skeleton

You Need:
• 2 hula hoops   • tape
• orange crepe paper

Loop the Hoop

Before the party:
• Wrap the hula hoops with orange crepe paper and secure with tape.

1. Form 2 circles.

2. Place a hula hoop on the arm of a student in each circle.

3. Everyone joins hands.

4. Loop each hoop around the circles without dropping hands. Students may step through the hoop or crawl through head first.

5. When the hoop has traveled around the entire circle, everyone sits down.

(This game is played relay style and is
a variation of the game Telephone.)

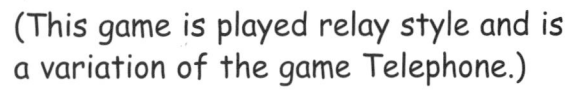

Spooky Face

1. Stand in two straight lines facing forward.

2. The last student in each line begins by tapping the player in front of them.

3. That player turns around and faces the tapper.

4. The tapper makes a spooky face.

5. The other player duplicates the spooky face, turns back toward the front and taps the student in front of him/her.

6. Now that student tries to mirror the spooky face.

7. Students continue trying to duplicate the spooky face shown them until the beginning of the line has been reached.

8. The first and last student in line show the class their spooky face to see how close they match.

Before the Party:
- Reproduce and cut out a bone for each student using the pattern on page 116.
- Write a body part such as knee, skull, hand, arm, ankle, leg, foot, shoulder, back, or elbow on each bone (you may have duplicates.)

Funny Bones

1. Form a circle. Give each student a bone.

2. One player begins by reading the word on their bone.

3. The next player reads the word on their bone and the two players connect their actual body parts.

4. Continue around the circle connecting body parts until the entire class has linked their funny bones.

A Haunting Tale

Before the Party:
- Sprinkle flour to resemble dust in and around the outside of the closed book.
- Cover with cobwebs.

Begin the party by telling the students this tale:

"One Halloween night many years ago when I was a child just about your age, I went out trick or treating with my friends. We stumbled upon an eerie looking mansion. We were a bit curious as to what kinds of treats would be given away so we headed up to the doorway. A servant named (your principal's name) answered the door and invited us into the old library. (Principal's name) told us that for our treat we could pick out any book off the bookshelf. We quickly grabbed the first book we could and rushed out of that spooky old place. I hadn't thought about that book for all these years until I stumbled upon it the other day. I thought you might enjoy looking at it. (Pick off the cobwebs, open the book and blow off the dust. Cough for effect and pause a moment as if reading something very important. Gasp loudly!) WOW! This is no ordinary book. This is a book full of spells. It says in here that fairies use this book to cast spells of good fortune on all who read from the book. Let's see if there is a spell in here for Halloween. (Thumb through the pages.) We are in luck! There is a Halloween spell and it goes like this:"

"Clap your hands twice,
and smile really nice.
Turn all around,
and touch the ground.
Shout out "Boo"
and the very best party
will be granted to YOU!"

"Let's say the spell together."
(Say the spell and do the actions together. Slam the book shut.)
"HAPPY HALLOWEEN! Let's begin the party and see if the spell works!"

Halloween Team Builders

These team builders are designed to form four groups of students.
Make quantity adjustments according to the number of students in your class.

Dot to Dot

You Need:
* 4 different colored dot stickers

1. Stand in a circle.

2. Place a sticker on each student's forehead making sure they don't see the sticker's color.

3. Each student pairs up with the person next to them and asks them 3 questions that will help determine the color of dot on their forehead. The questions may NOT contain a color word. For example:

   Does the color of my sticker rhyme with bed?
   Is my sticker the color of grass?
   Am I wearing the color of my sticker on my shirt?

4. After the students guess their colors, connect the dots by getting into groups of the same color.

You Need:
* stickers of 4 different types of farm animals

Barnyard Bash

1. Place a sticker in the palm of each student's hand.

2. Say "cock-a-doodle-doo!" and students begin to make the sound of the animal on their sticker.

3. Form groups by finding other students making the same sound.

Let's Face It

You Need:
- orange construction paper

Before the Party:

- Cut out small orange pumpkins, one for each student.
- Write an emotion on each shape, such as happy, sad, mad, afraid.
- To form four groups of six students, write four different emotions six times, each on a separate pumpkin.

1. Give each student a pumpkin.

2. Students pretend they are jack-o-lanterns and make expressions on their faces that show the emotion written on their pumpkins. No speaking allowed.

3. Students find others expressing the same emotion to form their station groups.

You Need:
- slips of paper

Hum That Tune

Before the Party:

- To form four groups, write down the names of four popular songs on as many pieces of paper that you want players in a group.   Song examples:

    "Twinkle, Twinkle, Little Star"
    "Mary Had a Little Lamb"
    "London Bridge"
    "Happy Birthday"

1. Give each student a slip of paper.

2. Say "hum," and students begin humming the tune of the song written on their paper.

3. Children find others humming the same tune to form their station groups.

Shake It Up

You Need:
- small pieces of paper with the numbers 1,2,3, or 4 written on each
- plastic pumpkin

1. Place the numbered papers in the pumpkin.

2. Students sit in a circle, pass the pumpkin around, and draw out one number.

3. Say "shake it up!" and students move around shaking hands with other players. Each student can only pump hands up and down as many times as the number written on their paper. Without speaking, students try to find others who have the same number.

4. When players find similar hand shakers, they link arms together and form a group. Continue until the teams are formed.

You Need:
- blank name tags
- markers

Character Building

Before the Party:
- Write the names of characters from four popular children's books on name tags.

Examples:	
Charlotte's Web	*Charlotte, Templeton, Wilber, Fern, Mr. Zuckerman, Avery*
The Boxcar Children	*Henry, Jessie, Violet, Benny, Grandfather, Watch*
The Cat In The Hat	*Sally, Thing 1, Thing 2, the fish, Mother, the Cat*
Wizard of Oz	*Dorothy, Toto, Scarecrow, Tin Man, Cowardly Lion, Wicked Witch*

1. Give each child a name tag to stick on their shirt.

2. Students find other characters from the same book and form their station groups.

Halloween Games

These games have been designed to play with small groups of students.

Zinger

Before the Party:
- Write each name on a lunch bag.

1. Place a variety of small prizes on the tray. Have an additional supply ready to replace the prizes as needed.

2. Choose a student to leave the room.

3. The other students gather around the serving tray and select one prize to be the "zinger" item.

4. The student who left returns and begins to pick one prize at a time off the tray to put in their lunch bag. When the student chooses the item that was designated as the zinger, all the other students yell, "Z-Z-Z-Z!" The student keeps the prizes in their bag and their turn is now over.

5. Choose another student to leave the room, refill the tray, and continue the game until everyone has had a turn.

6. At the end of the game give additional prizes to those students who did not receive as many prizes as the student who chose the most.

Costumes in a Bag

You Need:
- large shopping bags, one per student in each group
- Halloween costumes or dress-up clothes
- music

Before the Party:
- Fill the bags with assorted costume pieces and accessories.

1. Place the bags in a circle.

2. Each child stands behind one bag.

3. Play music and instruct the students to walk around the circle of bags. When the music stops, each student takes one article of clothing from the bag closest to them and puts on the item.

4. Continue playing until the students are dressed in a wide variety of wacky costumes.

You Need:
- gummi worms
- black bowl or cauldron
- duct tape
- 2 paper cups per student, one labeled with their name
- high-backed chair

Wormy Witches Brew

(This is played much like the game of Drop the Clothespins.)

1. Give each child 10 worms in the cup that is not labeled.

2. Tape the cup that is labeled in the middle of the cauldron.

3. Position the cauldron behind the chair.

4. One at a time, a student kneels on the chair facing the chair's back.

5. Keeping hands above the chair back, the student drops their worms one at a time into the cauldron trying to fill their cup.

6. After each turn, the student keeps their cup full of wormy witches brew.

Boo Am I?

You Need:
- one round sucker per child
- white paper towel
- self-stick note pads
- insulated foam block
- ribbon

Before the Party:
- Wrap each sucker with a paper towel.
- Tie string below the candy sucker to form a ghost's head.
- Write a Halloween costume on the note paper.
  Suggested costumes: *ghost, firefighter, cowboy, dancer, princess, cat, monster*
- Stick the note to the sucker stick beneath the paper towel.
- Display the ghosts by sticking them into the foam block.

1. One child at a time chooses a ghost and silently reads the costume written under the ghost's skirt.

2. The student acts out the charade.

3. Whoever guesses the costume correctly chooses the next ghost and takes their turn acting out the charade.

4. When finished students keep their ghost suckers and the adult volunteer refills the foam block with more suckers for the next group.

You Need:
- wrapped candy, 10 pieces per student
- plastic pumpkins

Candy Catch

1. Divide students into pairs.

2. One student in each pair has a plastic pumpkin. The other student has ten pieces of candy.

3. One student throws the candy and the other student tries to catch it in their pumpkin. Keep what you catch. Leave the candy that drops on the floor.

4. Partners trade places and play again.

5. When everyone has had a chance to catch candy, make sure all players have 10 pieces of candy to keep.

Mystery Treats

You Need:
- 4 sets of 8 different types of candy, variety of shapes and sizes
- aluminum foil
- paper
- index cards, numbered 1 through 8
- pencils

Before the Party:
- Cover each item of candy with aluminum foil.

1. Place 8 wrapped candy items on a table and label each with a numbered card.

2. Hand out paper and pencil to each student.

3. Students number their papers 1 - 8.

4. Students try to guess the name of each candy by looking and touching the mystery treats.

5. Students write their guesses by the corresponding number on their answer sheets.

6. When all students have finished, carefully unwrap the candy to show the mystery treats.

7. Give each child one piece of candy and put another set of 8 wrapped candy pieces on the table for the next group.

You Need:
- an old white sheet

Boo Are You?

1. Form a circle.

2. Choose someone to be the ghost.

3. Cover the student with the sheet and help them leave the room.

4. Another student is then chosen to stand in the center of the circle.

5. The ghost is escorted back in the room and tries to guess who is in the middle of the circle by asking only yes or no questions such as, "Are you a girl?" or "Do you wear glasses?"

6. The student in the middle can disguise their voice when answering the questions.

7. After the person is named, someone else takes a turn.

Vanishing Ghosts

You Need:
- chalk
- water
- sponges
- cotton balls
- chalkboard
- dry cloth or towels

1. All students at the station draw an outline of a ghost on the chalkboard, then shade in its body using the side of their chalk. (Place kids appropriately apart.)

2. Students move back about 5 feet from the board.

3. Give each student 3 wet cotton balls, squeezed fairly dry.

4. Say "boo!" and students throw 1 cotton ball at a time at the board making eyes and a mouth for their ghost.

5. When finished, give students additional wet cotton balls to throw at their ghost to help it "vanish."

6. Wash and dry the chalkboard before the next group begins.

You Need:
- inflated long balloons, one per team
- masking tape

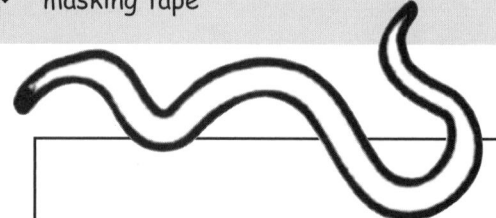

Take the Snake

1. Divide the group into 2 equal teams.

2. Mark a beginning line and a turn around line using masking tape.

3. Have each team line up.

4. The first player in each line places the snake (balloon) between their legs.

5. Say "slither!" and players run down to the turn around line and back to the beginning line trying to keep the snake between their legs.

6. When players get back to their next teammate, the new player takes the snake between their legs without using their hands.

7. Continue the relay until everyone has had a chance to play.

Waiter Walk

You Need:
* serving trays, one per team
* inflated white balloons
* masking tape

1. Divide your group into equal teams.

2. Mark a beginning line and a turn around line using masking tape.

3. Give a tray to the first person in each team.

4. Place a ghost (balloon) on each tray.

5. Each person walks to the turn around line and back again with the tray held high above their head like a waiter. Students must walk carefully so their ghost doesn't float away. If the ghost falls off, the student picks it up and puts it back on the tray before continuing to walk.

6. Play continues until all have had a chance to do the waiter walk.

You Need:
* 3 pounds spaghetti noodles
* 2 large plastic bowls
* plastic spider rings, one for each student
* masking tape

Gooey Guts

<u>Before the Party:</u>
* Cook spaghetti noodles and drain.
* Place the noodles in 2 large bowls.
* Hide rings in the spaghetti.

1. Divide the group into two teams.

2. Mark a beginning line and turn around line using masking tape.

3. Place the spaghetti bowls at a turn around spot for each team.

4. The first students run down to the bowls and dig in the "guts" until they find spider rings.

5. Students put the rings on their fingers and run back to tag the next person in line. Continue until everyone has a ring. (Students will need to wash after this activity.)

Trick for a Treat

You Need:
- plastic knives and forks
- plastic pumpkins or bowls, 1 for each team
- wrapped miniature candy bars

1. Fill the plastic pumpkins with candy bars and set the pumpkins away from the students on a table or desks.

2. Divide the group into equal teams and line up as in a relay.

3. Give the first person in each line a set of plastic silverware.

4. Say "trick or treat!" and the first student in each line runs to the pumpkins and picks out one piece of candy using only their utensils.

5. Next, the students place the candy on the table and unwrap it using only their plastic silverware. No hands allowed! Once the candy is unwrapped the students may use their hands to eat their treat.

6. Students then run back to their teammates and give them the set of silverware. The game continues until all have had the chance to play.

You Need:
- medium-sized pumpkin for each student in the group
- shaving cream   - black permanent marker
- paper towels   - newspaper
- razors, with the blades removed

Shave Jack

Before the Party:
- Draw a face on each pumpkin using the marker.

1. Set each pumpkin on newspaper.

2. Squirt shaving cream in students' hands.

3. Students smooth the cream on the pumpkin forming a beard and mustache.

4. Using the razors, students now have fun shaving Jack.

5. Have paper towels available to wipe off hands and razors.

Bat the Bat

You Need:
- 7" black paper plates
- black electrical tape
- black construction paper
- inflated black balloons
- masking tape
- tongue depressors
- rulers

Before the Party:
- Make 1 bat per team.
- Cut out 2 wings using pattern on page 118, from black construction paper and tape them to the back side of the paper plate.
- Tape a tongue depressor to the back of the plate to be used as a handle.

1. Mark a beginning line and a turn around line using masking tape.

2. Divide the students into equal teams and line up as in a relay.

3. The first student on each team uses the paper plate bat to hit the balloon and keep it from landing on the ground while they are walking to the turn around line and back again.

4. The game continues until all have had a chance to bat the bat.

You Need:
- ping pong balls
- permanent markers
- masking tape
- straws

Rolling Eyeballs

Before the Party:
- Turn 1 ping pong ball per team into an eyeball by using permanent markers. Draw an iris and a pupil on the ball, then add red lines to show bloodshot eyes.

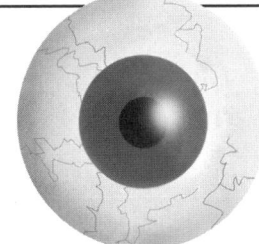

1. Mark a beginning line and a turn around line using masking tape.

2. Divide into equal teams and form a line for each team. Give each child a straw.

3. The first person in each line kneels and places the eyeball in front of them.

4. Say "blink!" and the players blow through the straw and move their eyeball down to the turn around line. After crossing the line they pick up the ball and carry it back to their teammates. (This playing field should be fairly short so the students don't get light headed.)

5. Continue playing until all have had the chance to roll the eyeball.

Ghost Bowling

Before the Party:
- Paint the pop bottles white to represent ghosts.
- Pour a little rice in the bottom of each for added weight.

1. Set up the pop bottles as you would bowling pins.

2. Use a small pumpkin as the bowling ball.

3. Taking turns, students roll two times to knock down as many ghost pins as possible.

Pin the Face on the Jack-o-Lantern

Before the Party:
- Using yellow construction paper, cut out several different jack-o-lantern eyes, noses, and mouths.
- Outline a large orange pumpkin on the chalkboard.

1. Students choose one jack-o-lantern face part.

2. Place a piece of double stick tape on the back of each facial feature.

3. Blindfold the first student, turn them around 3 times, and place them in front of the pumpkin on the board.

4. The student tapes their face part to the pumpkin.

5. When each student has helped make the jack-o-lantern's face, give them all a piece of paper and crayons to draw and color their crazy jack-o-lantern creation.

Candy Corn Craze

You Need:
* candy corn
* masking tape
* bowls

1. Divide the group into 2 equal teams.

2. Mark a beginning line and a turn around line using masking tape.

3. The first player on each team picks out a piece of candy corn from the bowl.

4. The students place the candy corn on the back of their hands and run down to the turn around line. Once there, they must flip the candy corn into the air and catch it with the same hand.

5. The students then place the candy corn on the back of their other hand and run back to the beginning.

6. If the candy falls students pick it up, place it back on their hand, and continue the race.

You Need:
* witch hat * broom
* chairs

Witch's Seat Scramble

Before the Party:
Arrange the chairs in a circle using as many chairs as there are players, minus one. Chairs should face toward the inside of the circle.

1. Practice this chant a few times with all the students.
I am a witch, who's looking for a seat.
When I call your names, jump to your feet.

2. One student is chosen to be the witch and is given the hat and broom. The witch stands in the center of the circle and says the chant, then calls out the names of two players in the circle.

3. The players whose names are called try to exchange seats as the witch also tries to sit in one of their chairs.

4. The player left without a chair takes the broom and hat and becomes the new witch.

5. Play continues until everyone has had their name called.

The Mad Lab

You Need:

- doctor's lab jacket
- plastic tablecloth
- Halloween mask
- 8 pails or bowls
- paper towels
- large dog bone - (leg)
- rubber glove, filled with sand - (hand)
- candy corn - (teeth)
- small balloon, filled with water - (heart)
- peeled grapefruit - (brain)
- cooked and drained spaghetti - (intestines)
- cherry tomatoes or black olives - (eyeballs)
- 8 lunch bags
- scissor
- pencils
- clipboards
- paper
- wig - (hair)

Before the Party:

- Set up your mad lab by placing 8 bowls on a table and covering the table with the tablecloth.
- Cut slits above each bowl, just large enough for a child's hand to slip through.
- Label each opening with a number.
- Place the mask at the top of the sheet to resemble a patient.
- Immediately before the party, fill the bowls with the lab items.

1. The facilitator of this game dresses up as a mad scientist.

2. Students enter the mad lab and stand by a number.

3. The facilitator begins the game by telling this story:
"The crazy Dr. Stein N. Frank has a reputation for getting everything mixed up. The poor person lying here came to see the doctor for an operation. While performing the surgery Dr. Stein N. Frank removed body parts then lost his glasses and now can't identify which part is which. It is your job as assistant doctors to poke and prod and see if you can correctly identify the parts the doctor removed. You will each be given a clipboard and paper and pencil. Number your paper 1 - 8. After feeling inside each opening, write the body part you think Dr. Stein N. Frank removed next to the corresponding number on your paper.

4. Students slip one hand inside the numbered opening they are standing beside and imagine which body part they could be touching. Students write their guess on their paper.

5. Have paper towels available to wipe off hands.

6. Students rotate around the table until all body parts have been explored.

7. Discuss and compare students' answers with the facilitator.

The Great Pumpkin Hunt

You Need:
- orange paper pumpkins
- candy treats
- plastic pumpkin

Before the Party:
- Make paper pumpkins and write clues on them for the students to solve.
- Place the clues in the appropriate spots.
- Fill a plastic pumpkin with candy treats and hide it in the place where your final clue leads.

Suggested clues:

Clue 1: *Reading is a fun thing to do.*
Can you guess where you will find clue #2? (library)

Clue 2: *Go to the room with many kids in a bunch,*
Laughing and talking and eating their lunch. (cafeteria)

Clue 3: *The person who is our leader at school,*
Works in a place that is really cool. (principal's office)

Clue 4: *The pumpkin will be in a big, large place,*
Where kids are allowed to run and race. (gym)

1. Read the first clue in the classroom.

2. Students follow the clues and go on their great pumpkin hunt with an adult.

3. The last clue should lead the students to the plastic pumpkin filled with treats.

4. Each student may select one treat.

5. After reading each clue, leave it in place for the other groups that have not yet gone on their great pumpkin hunt.

Boo Who?

You Need:
- plastic liter bottle
- white and black paint
- slips of paper

Before the Party:

- Paint the bottle to look like a ghost.
- Write phrases of things children may do or see on Halloween and place them in the ghost.

Suggestions:

a mad scientist experimenting	*carving a pumpkin*
playing games at a Halloween party	*a bat flying*
a witch flying on a broomstick	*a bat sleeping*
walking through a haunted house	*opening candy*
getting dressed into a costume	*trick-or-treating*

1. Students sit in a circle.

2. Place the ghost on its side in the middle of the circle.

3. Students take turns spinning the ghost.

4. Whomever the ghost is pointing to when it stops takes out one slip of paper.

5. The student pantomimes the idea and the others guess the Halloween action.

6. After spinning, if the ghost faces someone who has already had a turn, spin again.

7. When finished, return all ideas to the ghost so the next group can play.

Halloween Crafts

Quantities should be determined by the number of students at each station.

Bony Bodies

You Need:
- cotton swabs
- glue
- 9" x 12" black construction paper
- white paper
- black marker

Before the Party:
- Cut off the ends of some cotton swabs. Cut other swabs in half and leave some swabs full length.

1. Cut a skull shape from the white paper. Draw a face using the black marker.

2. Glue the skull to the top of the black paper.

3. Arrange cotton swabs on the black paper then glue them down to form a skeleton.

4. Lay flat to dry.

Pumpkin Pals

You Need:
- craft glue
- orange poster board
- 9" round orange balloon
- assorted craft items such as yarn, lace, buttons, sequins, wiggle eyes, tissue paper, felt-tipped markers, feathers

Before the Party:
- Cut 8" heart shapes from poster board.
- Cut a slit in the pointed end, 1/3 of the way up towards the center of the heart.

1. Blow up a balloon and knot.

2. Slide the knot through the heart slit.

3. Decorate facial features on the balloon using an assortment of craft supplies and glue.

Spooktacular Spooks

You Need:
- wire hangers
- white knee-high nylon stockings
- rubber bands
- black felt-tipped markers
- ribbon

1. Bend a hanger into a ghost shape.

2. Beginning at the hanger base, stretch the stocking over the hanger.

3. Use a rubber band to secure the top of the nylon to the hanger head.

4. Draw a spooky face on the nylon using the marker.

5. Tie ribbon around the rubber band to decorate.

You Need:
- clothespins
- black foam sheet
- craft glue
- adhesive magnetic strip
- wiggle eyes
- poster board
- scissors
- Halloween ribbon

Creepy Clips

Before the Party:
- Cut magnetic strip into 3" lengths.
- Cut bat tracers from poster board using the pattern on page 116.

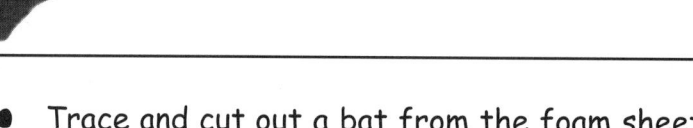

1. Trace and cut out a bat from the foam sheet.

2. Glue the foam shape on the clothespin making sure the clip end points down.

3. On the back of the clothespin, attach a magnetic strip.

4. Decorate the creepy clip with eyes and ribbon.

Flying Ghosts

You Need:
- 9" x 12" white construction paper
- paper punch
- black marker
- pencil
- white yarn, cut in 20" lengths
- scissors

1. Trace your foot on white paper and cut it out.

2. Punch a hole through the toes of the foot.

3. Thread a strand of yarn through the hole and tie.

4. Draw a ghost's face on each side of the foot.

You Need:
- 12" x 18" black construction paper
- cotton balls
- glue
- stapler
- black marker

I Spy Spider Headband

Before the Party:
- For each student cut 2 black 3" x 18" strips and 8 black 1" x 9" inch strips.

1. Staple two long paper strips together, then fit it around the student's head. Staple it to form a headband.

2. Fold 8 smaller paper strips accordion style to use as the spider's legs.

3. Staple the legs to the inside of the headband.

4. Draw pupils on 2 cotton balls.

5. Glue the cotton balls on the headband to form the spider's eyes.

Spider Webs

You Need:
- plastic forks
- white construction paper
- black felt-tip markers
- black stamp pads
- shirt box
- bowl
- marbles
- black paint

1. Place white paper on the bottom of the box.

2. Pour black paint into the bowl.

3. Dip the marble in the bowl of paint.

4. Using a fork take the marble from the paint and shake off any excess.

5. Place the marble in the box.

6. Shake the box from side to side.

7. Repeat steps 3-6 until a web is made.

8. Remove the white paper from the box.

9. Press your thumb in a stamp pad to make fingerprint spider bodies in the web.

10. Using markers, finish the spiders by drawing legs on their bodies.

You Need:
- 12" x 18" orange poster board
- glue
- stickers

Pumpkin Peekers

Before the Party:
- Make poster board tracers using the glasses pattern on page 117.

1. Trace and cut glasses from orange poster board.

2. Decorate the glasses using stickers.

3. Bend the glasses so they tuck behind the ears.

Spider Writers

You Need:
- 1 1/2" styrofoam balls
- Halloween pencils   • scissors
- black pipe cleaners   • glue
- ball point pen   • mini wiggle eyes
- black spray paint

Before the Party:
- Spray paint the foam balls.

1. Using a pen, poke a hole in the styrofoam ball.

2. Poke the eraser end of the pencil into the hole.

3. Cut 2 pipe cleaners into 8 pieces.

4. Poke the pipe cleaners into the styrofoam and bend them to form spider legs.

5. Glue 2 eyes on the styrofoam to finish your spider writer.

You Need:
- baby food glass jars   • glue
- paint brushes   • bowls
- tea lights
- orange and black tissue paper

Jack-o-Lights

Before the Party:
- Cut orange tissue paper into 1" squares.
- Cut a variety of jack-o-lantern face pieces out of black tissue paper.

1. Mix glue and a few drops of water in the bowls.

2. Using a brush, paint glue on the outside of the jar.

3. Place orange tissue paper over the glue until the jar is completely covered.

4. Gently paint another coat of glue over the orange tissue paper.

5. Make a jack-o-lantern by gluing black tissue paper shapes on the jar to form the face.

6. Place a tea light in the jack-o-lantern.

7. Let dry.

Frightening Frank

You Need:
- green 8" x 10" party bags with handles
- black, red and white construction paper
- cotton balls
- mini paper muffin cups
- aluminum foil
- glue

1. Cut out 2 pupils from black paper and glue them to two cotton balls.

2. Glue the cotton balls inside two muffin cups.

3. Glue the muffin cup eyes on to the green bag.

4. Finish Frank's face by decorating with other materials.

5. Add aluminum foil monster bolts on the side of Frank's neck.

You Need:
- white plastic spoons
- orange and black yarn
- round suckers
- black permanent markers
- wiggle eyes
- white facial tissue
- glue

Spoon Spooks

1. Glue two eyes on the back side of a spoon.

2. Draw a spooky smile on the spoon using the marker.

3. Place the sucker in the front of the spoon and tie them together with a rubber band.

4. Wrap the tissue around the handle portion of the spoon and the sucker.

5. Tie everything together around the neck of the spoon using yarn.

Spooky Setting

You Need:
- large black paper plates
- white dinner napkins
- tag board
- margarine lids
- black and orange construction paper
- glue
- scissors
- tape

Before the Party:
- Make bat wing tracers from tag board using the pattern on page 118.
- Cut 1"x3" orange paper strips.

1. Trace and cut out bat wings on 12" x 18" black paper.

2. Cut out two triangle bat ears.

3. Glue wings and ears on the back of a paper plate to make a placemat.

4. Using the margarine lid, trace and cut out an orange circle.

5. Cut a jack-o-lantern face from black paper and glue it on the orange circle.

6. Tape the ends of an orange paper strip to the back of the jack-o-lantern circle to make a napkin holder.

7. Slide a napkin through the holder.

You Need:
- large, black 4-hole buttons
- black pipe cleaners
- mini wiggle eyes
- hot glue gun

Spider Rings

Before the Party:
- Cut pipe cleaners in fourths.

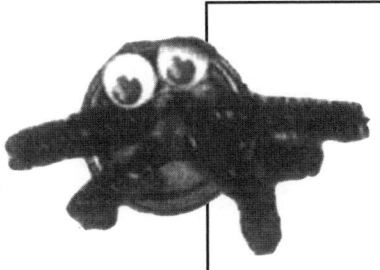

1. Thread one pipe cleaner through each button hole.

2. Bend the pipe cleaners in half to make eight legs.

3. Glue wiggle eyes on top of the button.

4. To make the ring, wrap two of the legs around a finger and twist together.

Pumpkin Pouch

You Need:
- orange and black fun foam
- paper punches
- thin, orange fabric ribbon or yarn
- assorted candy

Before the Party:
- Cut two pumpkin shapes of identical shape and size for each student from the orange fun foam.
- Measure and cut ribbon that is two times the circumference of the pumpkin.

1. Place two pumpkin shapes together.

2. Punch holes around both shapes leaving an opening at the top of the pumpkin.

3. Beginning at the top hole, sew the shapes together with the ribbon. Leave a length of ribbon at the beginning to tie together with the end to form a handle.

4. Cut out jack-o-lantern facial shapes from the black foam and glue them on the pumpkin to make a face.

5. Fill the pouch with candy.

You Need:
- 2" clay or plastic pots
- yellow, white and orange paint
- paint brushes
- candy corn

Corny Cups

Before the Party:
- Using a black marker, divide the pot into three parts.

1. Paint the pot to resemble a candy corn beginning with yellow paint on the lower third of the pot.

2. Let dry and fill with candy corn.

Silhouette Ghost

You Need:
- 9"x12" white and black construction paper
- white crayons
- scissors
- 1/8" black ribbon or yarn
- black marker
- large wiggle eyes
- white tissue paper
- glue

Before the Party:
- Cut white tissue paper into 8"x11" rectangles.
- Tie bows out of the ribbon.

1. Draw a ghost outline on black paper using a white crayon.

2. Beginning inside the ghost shape, cut out the ghost leaving the border intact.

3. Glue the tissue paper on top of a full sheet of white paper.

4. Glue the black construction paper border on top of the white tissue paper to make a silhouette.

5. Glue on wiggle eyes.

6. Draw a mouth and glue a tied bow on the neck.

You Need:
- 1 small pumpkin, not gourd
- colored ball-top pins
- craft items such as yarn, pipe cleaner, doll hair, eyes, gems, beads, lace, feathers, sequins

Crazy Pumpkins

Before the Party:
- Ask each student to bring a small pumpkin to school.

1. Decorate the pumpkins using pins to secure the craft items.

Halloween Treats

For ease and neatness we suggest students prepare their party treats on paper plates.

Peanut Butter Bugs

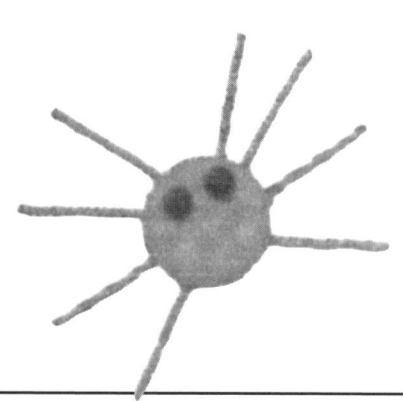

1. Spread peanut butter on 2 crackers.

2. Place pretzel sticks on one cracker to form legs.

3. Place second cracker on top of first.

4. Dab peanut butter on chocolate chips and place them on the top cracker for the bug's eyes.

Monster Mash Cupcakes

Before the Party:
- Use food coloring and dye the frosting green.

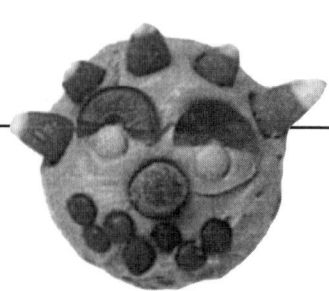

1. Spread frosting on a cupcake.

2. Create a monster using the assorted candy.

Ghosts to Gobble

You Need:
- creme-filled golden sponge cakes
- plastic knives
- whipped cream
- candy corn
- black gel frosting

1. Spread whipped cream over the sponge cake.

2. Using black gel, draw a ghost face.

3. Place 2 candy corns below the ghost's head to form a bow tie.

You Need:
- double stuffed chocolate sandwich cookies
- black shoestring licorice, cut into short pieces
- chocolate chips
- black gel icing

Double Stuffed Spiders

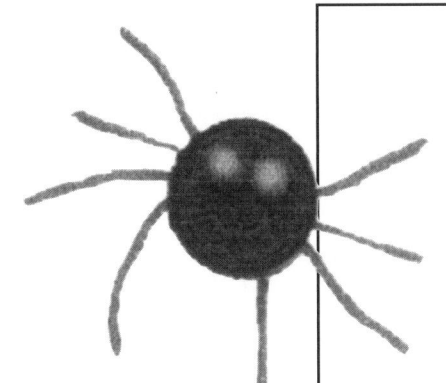

1. Twist the cookie open.

2. Cross 4 pieces of licorice on one cookie half to make legs.

3. Put the top back on the cookie.

4. Using gel icing, glue the chocolate chips on the cookie for the spider's eyes.

Nummy Mummies

You Need:
- mozzarella cheese sticks
- 8" soft tortilla shells
- pizza sauce
- microwave

1. Wrap the cheese stick with the tortilla shell to resemble a mummy.

2. Microwave for 15-20 seconds until cheese melts.

3. Dip in pizza sauce.

Worm Pudding

You Need:
- chocolate pudding cup
- gummi worms
- sandwich bags
- spoons
- chocolate sandwich cookies
- foil-wrapped pumpkin chocolate candy

1. Place 2 cookies in a sandwich bag.

2. Crush the cookies using your hands.

3. Open the pudding and put the crumbs on top of the pudding to resemble dirt.

4. Add worms crawling from the dirt.

5. Top with a wrapped pumpkin chocolate candy.

You Need:
- pretzel rods
- white crayons
- white frosting
- candy corns
- black paper plates
- plastic knives

Finger Food

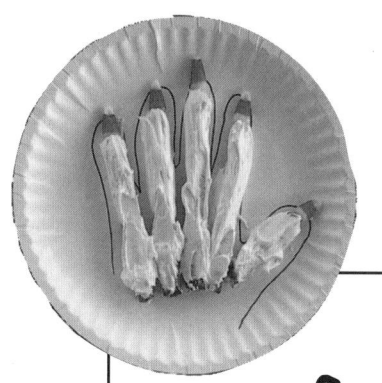

1. Trace your hand on the paper plate using a crayon.

2. Frost the pretzel rods with white frosting.

3. Arrange 5 pretzel rods in the finger outlines.

4. Place candy corns at the ends of the pretzels to form nails.

Goblin Grins

1. An adult slices the apple into wedges, 2 per student.

2. Spread peanut butter on both slices.

3. Press marshmallows on one apple slice to form teeth.

4. Place the apple slices together to make a grin.

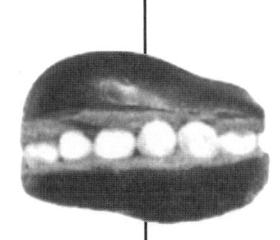

Krispy Pumpkin Pops

1. Unwrap both cereal bars.

2. Mold the cereal bars into one pumpkin shape.

3. Push a craft stick into the pumpkin.

4. Make a jack-o-lantern face by pressing candies in the pumpkin head.

Orange Floats

Before the Party:
- Snip both ends off the licorice.

1. Put 2 scoops of sherbet in a large drinking cup.

2. Pour orange soda over the sherbet.

3. Use the licorice as a straw.

4. Eat with a spoon.

Witch Hats

You Need:
- fudge striped cookies
- chocolate frosting
- colored sugar sprinkles
- sugar cones
- plastic knives

1. Spread frosting on one cookie.

2. Place a cone upside down on the cookie.

3. Spread frosting over the top half of the cone.

4. Decorate the hat by sprinkling colored sugar over the cone.

You Need:
- powdered sugar donuts
- gummi candy circles
- chocolate chips
- red gel icing

Edible Eyes

1. Place a gummi candy circle covering the hole in the donut.

2. Using red gel frosting, glue a chocolate chip in the center of the candy ring.

3. Form blood shot eyes by adding lines of red gel icing on the donut.

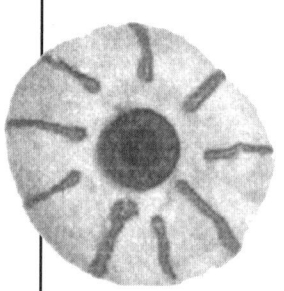

Breadstick Bones

You Need:
- refrigerated bread stick dough
- spaghetti sauce   • bowls
- cookie sheets lined with aluminum foil
- permanent marker   • oven

1. Give students one strip of dough.

2. Tie knots at both ends of the dough to resemble a bone.

3. Place the dough on the cookie sheet and write the students' names on the foil.

4. Follow the directions on the package to bake.

5. Dip in spaghetti sauce.

Snacks With Jack

You Need:
- round, orange deli cheese slices
- thinly sliced summer sausage
- assorted crackers
- plastic knives

1. Cut jack-o-lantern face shapes out of summer sausage.

2. Place the meat shapes on the cheese slice to build a face.

3. Eat with crackers.

You Need:
- chocolate, cream-filled cupcakes
- black licorice   ◆ red hots
- gel icing

Black Widow Delights

1. Place a cupcake upside down on a paper plate.

2. Cut four licorice pieces in half.

3. Form spider legs by poking the licorice into the cupcake.

4. Use gel icing to glue red hots on the cupcake to make eyes.

Monster Dew

You Need:
- cans of pop
- green construction paper
- craft glue
- assorted craft items such as yarn, stickers, lace, ric-rac, wiggle eyes, pipe cleaners
- transparent tape
- straw

Before the Party:
Cut green paper to fit the pop cans.

1. Tape green paper around a pop can.

2. Turn the can into a monster by gluing on craft items.

3. Open the can and drink with a straw.

Prize Pumpkins

You Need:
- English muffins, split in half
- pizza sauce
- pizza toppings such as pepperoni, shredded mozzarella cheese, black olives, green peppers
- plastic knives
- oven or toaster oven

1. Spread pizza sauce on an English muffin half.

2. Add toppings to make a pizza pumpkin.

3. Heat in the oven at 375° for 10 minutes or until cheese melts.

You Need:
- fudge-striped cookies
- white frosting
- green food coloring
- chocolate candy kisses
- creme-filled golden sponge cakes
- peanuts in a shell
- shoestring licorice
- assortment of small candies
- plastic knives

Wacky Witches

Before the Party:
- Dye the frosting green.

1. Frost a sponge cake with green frosting.

2. Decorate the witch's face with assorted candy. Use a peanut for the nose.

3. Make hair using licorice.

4. Unwrap a kiss.

5. Dab a small amount of frosting in the center of the cookie and place a kiss on the frosting to form a witch's hat. Put the hat on the witch's head.

The following recipes can be prepared prior to the party.

Pops"ick"les

You Need:
- gummi snacks such as worms, bugs, reptiles, etc.
- 3 oz. paper cups
- green juice
- craft sticks
- aluminum foil

1. Place gummi snacks in the bottom of the cup.

2. Fill the cup full with juice.

3. Cover the cup with aluminum foil.

4. Cut a slit in the foil and push the craft stick through the slit. Freeze.

5. Take the treat out of the freezer a few minutes before serving.

6. Remove the foil and the pops"ick"les will pop out of the cup.

Ghoul-Aid

You Need:
- ginger ale
- large witch's cauldron
- surgical glove (non-powdered)
- clear plastic cups
- gummi worms
- cranberry juice
- string

1. Wash the glove inside and out.

2. Fill the glove with cranberry juice, tie, and freeze.

3. When ready to serve, fill the cauldron with ginger ale.

4. Add gummi worms or other edible ghoulish items.

5. Cut the glove off the frozen juice and place the hand in the cauldron and serve.

Winter Mixers

A mixer is the kick-off activity to the party. It involves the entire class, building excitement for the party and setting the stage for fun.

Give A Cheer, Winter's Here

1. Stand in a large circle.

2. The first student jumps in the circle shouting their name and performing an action.

3. Next, the entire class jumps forward and imitates their classmate.

4. Then, everyone jumps back.

5. Continue around the circle until everyone has had a chance to introduce themselves with a cheer.

Kids' Crawl

1. Students stand in a single file line with their feet spread wide so their classmates can crawl through them. (A hallway would work well.)

2. The last player in line begins crawling through the leg tunnel.

3. After the player has crawled under about five students, the next student begins crawling through the tunnel.

4. As each student reaches the beginning of the line and pops out of the tunnel, they shout "_____(their name)'s out!"

5. Remind the students to keep standing with their feet apart until all children have crawled through the entire tunnel.

The Elves and the Shoemixer

1. Students take off one shoe and put it in a pile in the middle of the room.

2. Divide the class into two groups.

3. Place each team on opposite sides of the room.

4. Say "go," and the students walk to the pile, find their shoes, put them on, and quickly walk back to their place.

5. When all players have their shoes back on and tied, the party "kicks" off.

You Need:
* pencils
* clipboards

Blizzard Buddies

Before the Party:
* Reproduce the Blizzard Buddies card on page 119.

1. Students walk around the room for approximately five minutes and ask their classmates a question from their blizzard card. If a student can answer yes, they should sign their name in the box.
Classmates can only sign each card once.

2. Say "freeze," and students stand still and take turns choosing a question and answer from their card to read out loud.

Polar Express

You Need:
- Polar Express written by Chris Van Alsburg
- white, red, blue, and green skeins of yarn
- bell

1. Read the book to the class.

2. Divide the class into four teams and have each team form a single file line.

3. Place the bell across the room from the four teams.

4. Give each team a skein of yarn.

5. Each team is going to turn itself into the Polar Express train. The first member of the team grasps the end of the yarn then hands the skein to the person behind them. This person pulls out more yarn, holds on to the strand, then passes the skein to the next person in line. Continue handing off the skein of yarn so it winds around the group ten times.

6. When the team is finished winding themselves together, they chug across the room to ring the sleigh bell.

Tobaggan Teamwork

You Need:
- 2 or 3 toboggans of the same size

1. Divide the class into two or three teams.

2. Teams line up behind each toboggan.

3. Say "look out below," and team members work together to add classmates, one by one, to their toboggan trying to fit everyone on. No body parts can touch the outside of the sled.

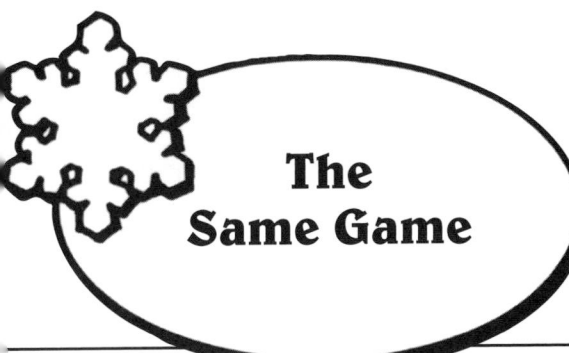

The Same Game

Before the Party:
Reproduce the word cards on page 120 and cut them apart.

happy

1. Give each student one word card.

2. Students form pairs by looking for the person who has a word that means the same as their word.

3. When everyone has found their partner, form a circle and share the synonyms.

glad

Counting Confetti

You Need:
- snowflake confetti
- plastic snack bags

Before the Party:
- Put 15-25 snowflakes in each student's snack bag.

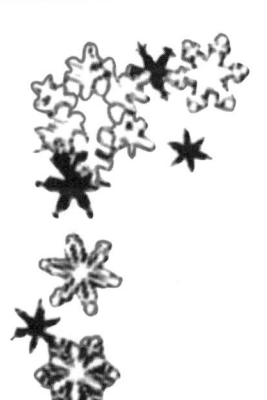

1. Give each student a bag of snowflakes.

2. Students pick out 0 to 3 pieces of confetti and enclose them in their right hand.

3. Students walk around the room and ask one classmate to guess the number of snowflakes they are holding in their hand. If the classmate guesses the correct amount of snowflakes, the snowflakes are given to the classmate with the correct answer. If the answer is not correct, no snowflakes are given to the classmate.

4. Students can change the amount of snowflakes in their hand each time they ask another student to guess.

5. Play the game for about 5 minutes. Students may keep any snowflakes they have collected at the end of the game.

Winter Team Builders

These team builders are designed to form four groups of students. Make adjustments according to the number of students in your class.

A Caroling We Will Go

<u>**Before the Party:**</u>
- On small slips of paper write the titles of four popular holiday songs. Each title will be written as many times as the number of students on each team. Suggested songs:
   "Jingle Bells"
   "Rudolph the Red-Nosed Reindeer"
   "We Wish You a Merry Christmas"
   "Frosty the Snowman"

1. Place the slips of paper in a bowl.

2. Each student chooses one slip of paper.

3. Say "sing," and everyone begins singing the song that is written on their paper.

4. Students form teams by finding other classmates who are singing the same song as themselves.

<u>You Need:</u>
- different flavored frozen ice bars, cut into bite-sized pieces.

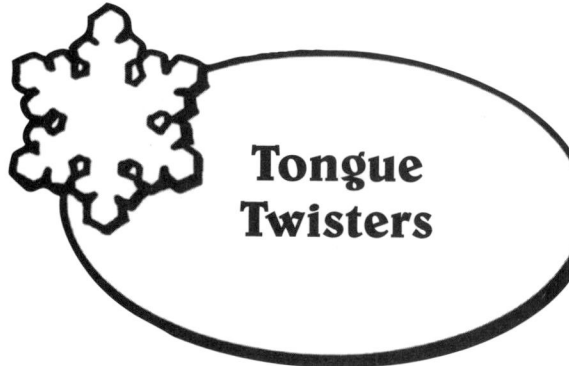

Tongue Twisters

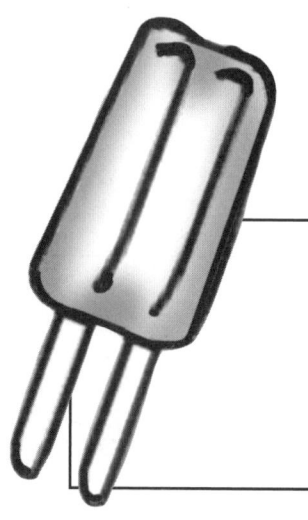

1. Students suck on a piece of ice bar until their tongues turn color.

2. Form groups by matching students with the same colored tongues.

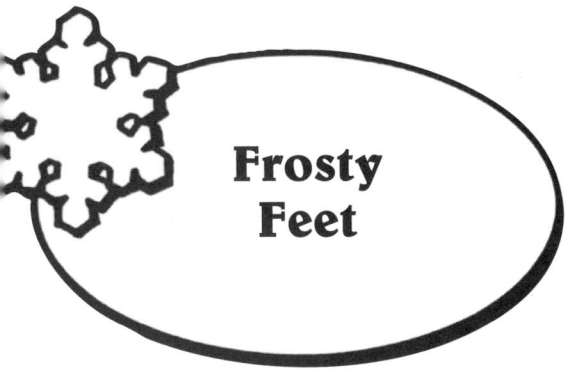

Frosty Feet

You Need:
- 4 different colored markers
- 3" x 3" self-stick notes

Before the Party:

- Choose four words associated with the winter season. The number of letters in each word should correspond with the number of students you want in each group.
  Suggested words for groups of six students:
  mitten, winter, skates, frosty
- Write one letter of each word on a sticky note using a different colored marker for each word.

1. Stick one letter on top of each child's shoe.

2. Students walk around and form teams by finding other students with letters of the same color.

3. Once a group is made, unscramble the winter word by standing in the correct order.

Finding Friends

1. An adult shouts out a number and the students form groups with as many members as the number called.

2. Continue three or four times, calling out different numbers, allowing students to form different groups.

3. The final number called should correspond with the number of students needed for each group.

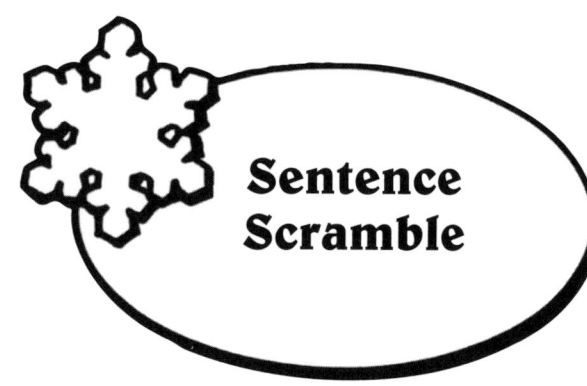

Sentence Scramble

You Need:
♦ 3" x 5" index cards

Before the Party:

- Think of four sentences with the number of words in each sentence corresponding with the number of students required for each group. No words should be repeated.

Suggested sentences for groups of six students:

I love winter because it snows.
Hot cocoa makes me warm inside.
Big snowmen are fun to build.
January is the year's first month.

1. Each child is given a word.

2. An adult calls out one sentence.

3. The students holding those words form a team and line up in the correct sentence order.

Before the Party:

- Write the names of instruments on small slips of paper.
  Suggested instruments:

  guitar
  keyboard
  trombone
  drum
  violin
  flute

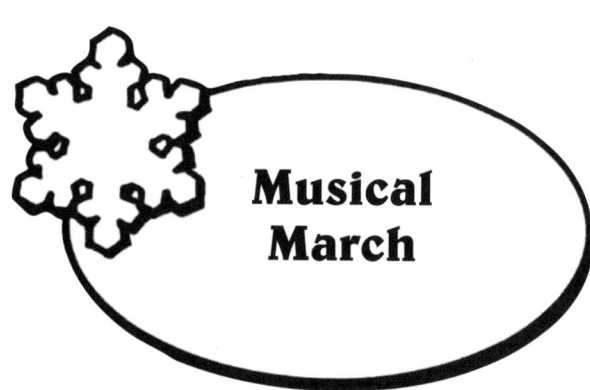

Musical March

1. Each child chooses a slip of paper.

2. Students pretend they are playing the instrument written on their paper while marching around the room.

3. Form groups by "directing" each instrument to a station.

Winter Games

These games have been designed to play with small groups of students.

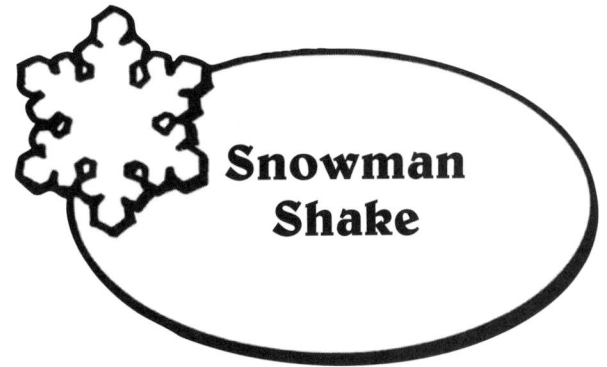

Snowman Shake

You Need:
- white, red, green, and black tag board
- dice
- 6 paper plates

Before the Party:
- Using the patterns on page 121, cut from tagboard one set of shapes for each student in the small group.
- Write the numbers 1 - 6 on paper plates.
- Put the snowman pieces on the corresponding plates.
  - 1 - large, white snowballs
  - 2 - medium, white snowballs
  - 3 - small, white snowballs
  - 4 - black eyes
  - 5 - red scarfs
  - 6 - green hats

1. Students will each try to build a snowman.
   To begin, a student must first roll a 1.
   If a 1 is rolled, the student takes one large snowman body piece from the plate labeled 1. The same student then rolls again trying to roll a 2. If a 2 is rolled the student takes the number 2 snowman piece.

2. If the correct number is not rolled in sequence, play passes to the next student.

Melting Snowballs

You Need:
- vanilla ice cream
- ice cream scoop
- paper plates

1. Place a scoop of ice cream on a paper plate.

2. This is a race to see who finishes their ice cream first. Say "lick," and students use only their tongues to lick their ice cream snowballs. No bites allowed.

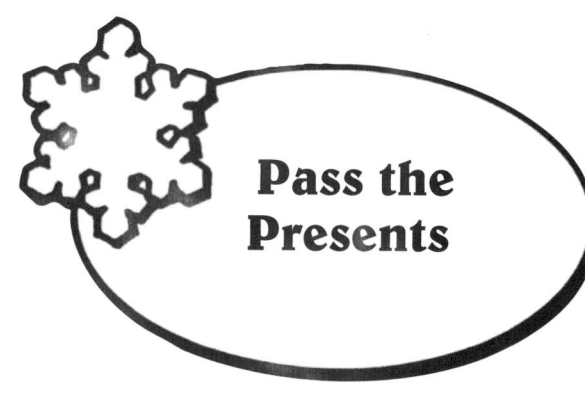

Pass the Presents

You Need:
- one shoe box per team
- variety of holiday wrapping paper
- holiday music

Before the Party:
- Fill each shoebox with prizes for all members on each team.
- Wrap the shoeboxes 4 or 5 times using different wrapping paper.

1. Students stand in a circle.

2. As the music begins playing, students pass the wrapped box around the circle.

3. When the music stops, the student who is holding the present carefully unwraps one layer of paper.

4. Continue playing until all the layers have been removed.

5. The last player holding the box, opens the lid and distributes the prizes to everyone in the group.

Frosty Fun

You Need:
- plastic top hat
- 3 tube socks
- duct tape

Before the Party:
- Turn the hat upside down and tape it to the floor.
- Make snowballs by rolling up the tube socks.

1. Students stand a predetermined distance from the hat.

2. Each student tries to toss the three snowballs into Frosty's hat.

3. Vary each round by having the students toss the snowballs from different distances, tossing them behind their backs, tossing them blindfolded, or tossing from under their legs.

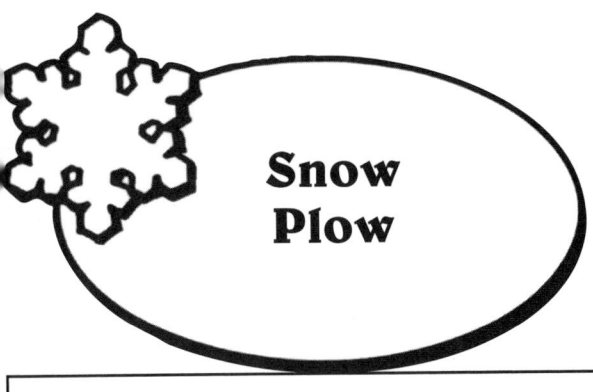

Snow Plow

You Need:
- small kitchen trash bags (one per team)
- straws
- cotton balls
- 2 bowls

Before the Party:
- Fill the trash bags with cotton balls.

1. Tell the students a snowstorm is coming and they are the snow plowers.

2. Students stand in a circle.

3. Place two bowls around the circle.

4. Give each student a straw.

5. Open one garbage bag and create a snowstorm by throwing out the cotton balls.

6. Students plow the snow by sucking up the cotton balls with their straws and dropping them into either bowl.

7. After 4-5 minutes the students freeze and count the number of snowballs they collected.

You Need:
- 2 tube socks

Sock It To Me

(This relay can be played with the entire class or in stations.)

Before the Party:
- Starting at the toe, roll each sock into a ball, then fold the opening of the sock around the sock ball.

1. Divide the students into two teams.

2. Students stand shoulder to shoulder and clasp their hands behind their backs.

3. The first student in each line tucks the snowball under their chin.

4. Say "sock it to me," and the students pass the snowballs to the students next to them using only their necks and chins, no hands.

Blizzard Blast

You Need:
- ream of inexpensive white paper
- masking tape

1. Divide the students into two equal teams.

2. Draw a center dividing line using the masking tape.

3. Each team lines up 6 feet from the center line.

4. Say "blizzard" and the teams smash up pieces of paper into snowball shapes and toss them across the center line. The goal is to throw more snowballs in your opponents' area than they throw into your area.

5. Students can also throw snowballs tossed into their area back to the opponents' area.

6. Say "freeze," and the storm is over and all players stop tossing snow.

7. Each team counts the number of snowballs on their side.

You Need:
- 2 pairs of mittens
- wrapped chocolate candy
- 2 bowls
- masking tape

Mitten Mischief

1. Mark a beginning line and a turn around line using masking tape.

2. Divide the group into two teams and each team lines up behind the beginning line.

3. Place the bowls filled with candy across the room.

4. The first student in each line wears a pair of mittens. Say "mitten mischief," and the students run to the bowls, unwrap a piece of candy, and pop it in their mouths.

5. Then, they run back to the next player and give them the mittens.

6. Play continues until everyone has had a turn.

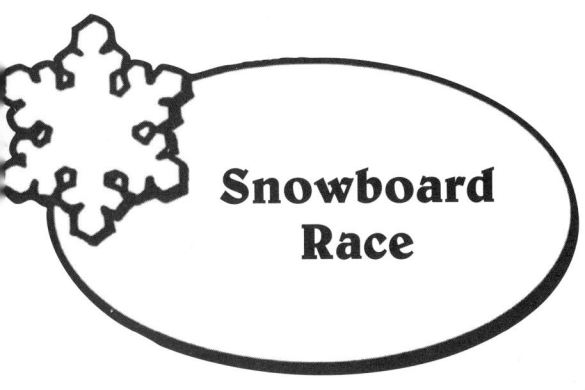

Snowboard Race

Before the Party:

- Duplicate the snowboard pattern on page 123 and make a blue snowboard for every student in the group.
- Write an action word on each snowboard making two identical sets of words. Suggested words: *gallop, skip, somersault, crawl, cartwheel, walk backwards, hop, crab walk*

1. Mark a beginning line and a turn around line using masking tape.

2. Divide the group into two teams.

3. Each team lines up behind the beginning line.

4. Place two identical piles of snowboards across the room.

5. Say "swoosh," and the first student in each team runs to their word pile, chooses a snowboard, and reads the word.

6. The student then performs the action back to the start line and tags the next player on the team.

7. Play continues until everyone has had a turn.

Stocking Stuffers

Before the Party:

- Using tape, tightly secure the stocking to the back side of the chair.

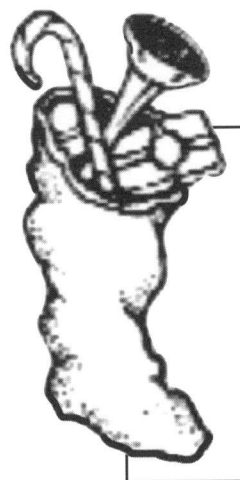

1. Give each student three candy canes.

2. One at a time, students stand on the chair and face the back of the chair.

3. Students try to drop each candy cane so it hooks and hangs on the edge of the stocking.

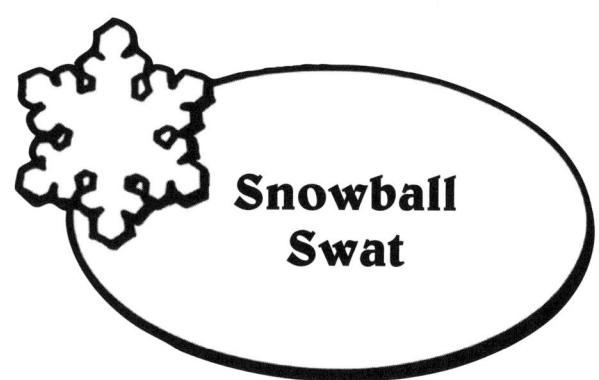

Snowball Swat

You Need:
- 2 wire clothes hangers
- 8 inflated white balloons
- 2 white knee-high nylons
- string
- masking tape

Before the Party:
- Bend circles out of the hangers.
- Beginning at the base of the circle, pull the nylons over each circle and tie around the base of the hanger hook using string.

1. Divide your group into two teams.

2. Mark a beginning line and a turn around line using masking tape.

3. Give the first player on each team a hanger swatter. Say "swat"," and the first person on each team hits the balloon with the swatter and keeps the balloon in the air while running down to the turn around line and back again. If the balloon touches the ground, students must start over.

4. At the end of each turn the students hand off the swatter and the balloon to the next player in line.

5. Play continues until all students have had a turn.

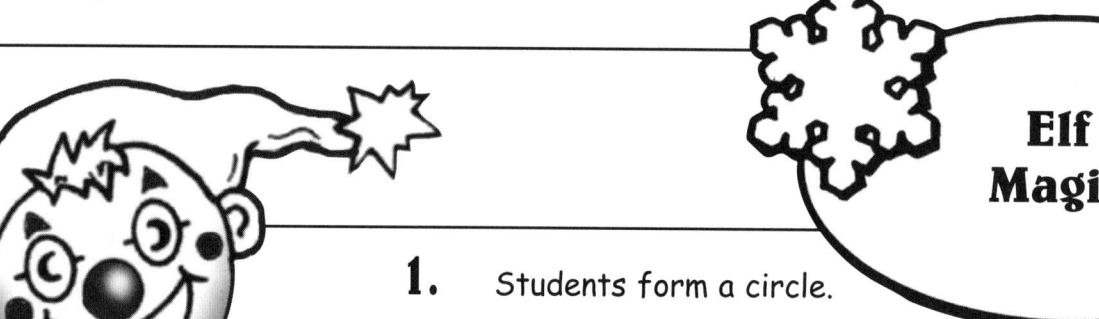

Elf Magic

1. Students form a circle.

2. Choose one student to leave the room and another to be the elf.

3. The elf begins a simple action such as clapping, winking, stomping, or clicking their tongue, and the other students imitate the action.

4. Invite the other student back in the room.

5. The elf tries to secretly change the action once the student is back and the student's job is to try and identify the elf.

6. Play again choosing others to be the student and the elf.

Blizzard Bowling

You Need:
- 10 plastic liter bottles
- plastic baseball
- white construction paper
- scorecard
- masking tape
- rice
- tape
- pencils
- funnel

Before the Party:
- Cover each bottle with white paper to represent snowmen.
- Fill the bottles with 1/2 cup rice.
- Duplicate the scorecards on page 122.
- Make a bowling lane using masking tape.

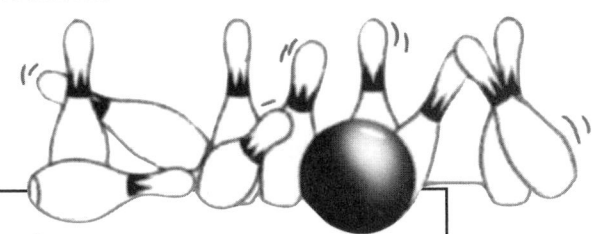

1. Set the bottles up in the formation of bowling pins.

2. Each student rolls the baseball twice trying to knock down the pins.

3. Students keep their scores on the scorecards.

4. Bowl as many frames as time allows.

You Need:
- holiday stocking
- paper plates
- toothpicks
- small pieces of paper
- play dough or clay

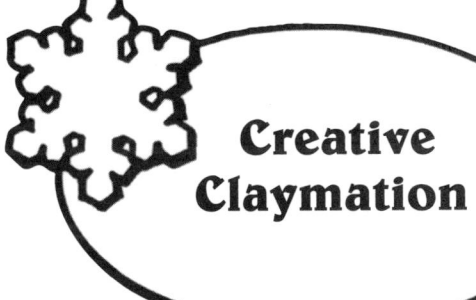

Creative Claymation

Before the Party:
- Write nouns associated with winter on slips of paper.
  Suggested nouns: *snowman, Santa, gift, bell, tree, stocking, ornament, candy cane, star*
- Fold and place paper slips in a stocking.

1. Give students a lump of clay on a paper plate.

2. Students choose a slip of paper from the stocking and mold the clay into the object written on their paper.

3. When finished have others guess the object that was made.

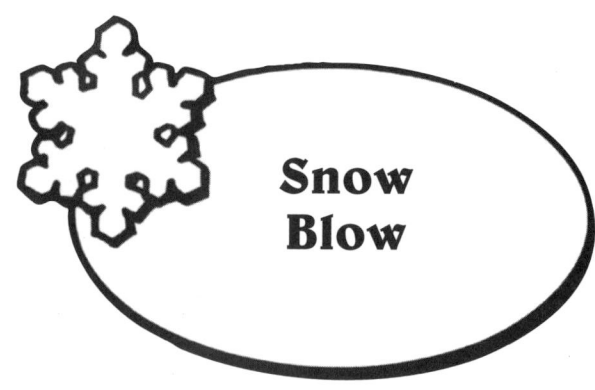

Snow Blow

You Need:
- ping pong ball
- index cards
- card table

Before the Party:
- Using one index card per letter, make two sets of cards that spell the word blizzard.

1. Divide the group into two teams.

2. Have the teams stand at each end of the card table.

3. Place the ping pong ball in the center of the card table.

4. The first player on each team tries to blow the ping pong snowball off the opposite end of the table. If the ball falls off the side of the table, pick it up and place it in the center again to start over.

5. The student that blows the ball off the end of the table earns a letter for their team.

6. The game is over when one team spells out the word blizzard.

You Need:
- 6 bean bags
- 2 bells
- string
- masking tape

Jingle Bells

Before the Party:
- Hang the bells from the ceiling.

1. Divide the students into two teams.

2. Mark a line on the floor to stand behind.

3. Taking turns, each student throws three bean bags and tries to ring the bell.

4. Keep score of how many times each team rings the bell.

Stuff For Stockings

You Need:
- 2 holiday stockings
- small gifts such as: pencils, notepads, apples, oranges, erasers, small cars, markers, crayons

1. Divide the group into two teams.

2. Place the stocking stuffers on a table across the room.

3. Give the first student on each team an empty stocking.

4. Say "stuff," and the student runs to the table and puts all the items in the stocking, then runs back to the next player in line.

5. The next player runs with the filled stocking back to the table, empties the stocking out, and takes it back to the next person in line.

6. Players continue filling and emptying the stocking until all students have had a chance to play.

7. After the game is over, ask the teams to list the items in the stocking without peeking. The stocking stuffers can then be given as prizes.

Snow Volleyball

You Need:
- 4 white inflated balloons ◆ yarn

Before the Party:
- Make the top of a net by taping yarn between two desks that are spread about 6 feet apart.

1. Divide the group into two teams.

2. Teams sit on the floor on each side of the net.

3. One student serves the ball by hitting the balloon over the net.

4. The opposing team tries to hit the balloon back.

5. Count the number of times the teams hit the ball over the net without it touching the ground. Try to improve the team's score each turn.

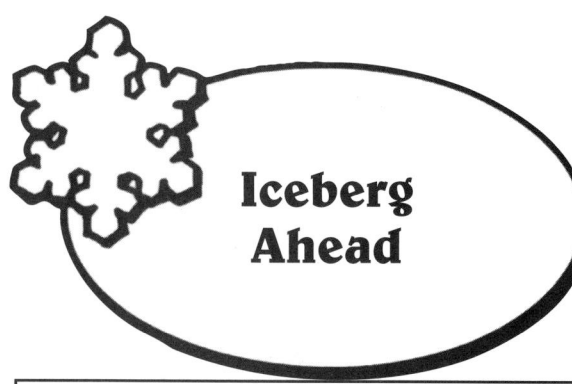

Iceberg Ahead

Before the Party:
- Cover the pop bottles with construction paper to resemble icebergs.

1. Set up two iceberg obstacle courses using the pop bottles.

2. Divide the students into two teams.

3. The first two students in a team, put a balloon between their stomachs and hold it there without using their hands.

4. Say "iceberg ahead," and the students maneuver their way through the iceberg obstacles and back again without dropping their balloon.

5. Play continues until everyone has had a chance to play.

You Need:
- 2 large plastic eggs
- rice
- masking tape

Penguin Play

Before the Party:
- Fill the eggs with rice, and tape the seams to prevent breaking.

1. Divide the students into two teams and form two lines.

2. Mark a beginning line and a turn around line using masking tape.

3. The first player in line places an egg on their feet. Balancing the egg by keeping heels together the players shuffle to the turn around line and back.

4. If the egg falls off, players put it back and continue shuffling.

5. Game continues until all have had a chance to play.

Abominable Snowman

You Need:
- 2 large white sweatshirts
- 2 laundry baskets
- 40 small white inflated balloons
- masking tape

1. Divide the group into two teams.

2. Make a turn around line using masking tape.

3. Choose one student on each team to be the abominable snowman and wear a sweatshirt.

4. Each team stands next to a laundry basket filled with 20 balloons.

5. Say "abominable," and each team stuffs the sweatshirt with the balloons from the basket.

6. When finished, the Abominable Snowman runs to the turn around line and back again.

Snow Scoop

You Need:
- bags of mini marshmallows
- 4 large plastic bowls
- 2 wooden spoons of the same size

1. Pour marshmallows into two bowls.

2. Divide the group into two teams and line up each team next to a filled bowl.

3. Put the two empty bowls across the room.

4. Give the first person on each team a wooden spoon. Say "scoop," and the players scoop as many marshmallows as they can on to the spoon without using their other hand.

5. Students race to the empty bowl, dump the marshmallows into the bowl, and race back to the starting point for the next person's turn. Marshmallows that fall may not be picked up.

6. When all have had a chance to play, count the the marshmallows to see which team scooped the most snow.

Snowball Bounce

You Need:
- flat sheet
- 1 different colored sock for each player

Before the Party:
- Roll the socks into balls.

1. Give each student a different colored snowball sock.

2. Students form a large circle and hold an edge of the sheet.

3. Say "bounce," and all students throw their snowballs on the sheet.

4. Students shake the sheet trying to bounce off their opponents' snowballs, while keeping their own snowball on the sheet.

5. If a snowball bounces off the sheet, play stops and the student whose snowball bounced off, steps back so the remaining students can rearrange themselves around the sheet and continue playing. Play continues until only one snowball remains.

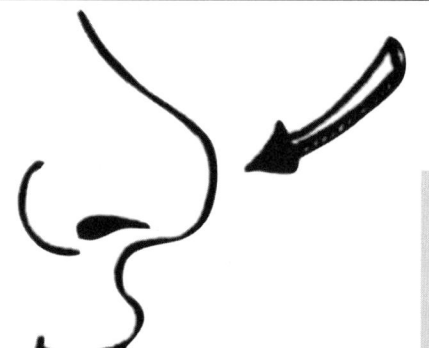

Snoseballs

You Need:
- 2 bowls
- mini marshmallows
- white tube frosting

1. Divide the students into two teams and line each group up in a single file.

2. Place two bowls of marshmallows across the room from the teams.

3. Squirt a nickel-sized amount of frosting onto everyone's noses.

4. Say "snoseball," and the first players run to the bowls, place their faces into the bowls and try to stick as many marshmallows as they can to the frosting on their noses without using their hands.

5. Players run back to the next team member. When everyone has had a chance to play, count the snoseballs that were collected by each team.

Winter Crafts

Quantities should be determined by the number of students at each station.

Santa Spoons

You Need:
- wooden spoons
- cotton balls
- red ribbon
- red permanent marker
- small red pompoms
- self-stick wiggle eyes

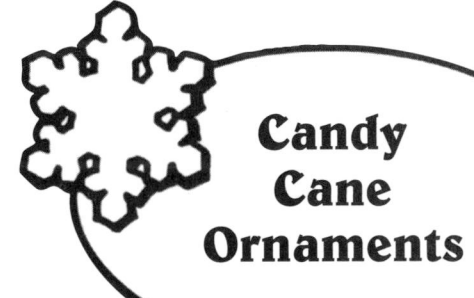

Before the Party:
- Drill a hole at the top of the spoon handle.
- Cut ribbon into 10" lengths.

1. Color the spoon handle and the top third of the spoon face red.

2. Glue a cotton ball at the bottom of the spoon face to form Santa's beard.

3. To make Santa's hat, glue one cotton ball to the end of the handle and glue more cotton where the red paint meets the face.

4. Stick two eyes on the spoon and glue a pompom on for the nose.

5. Loop ribbon through the hole and tie it so Santa can hang on a tree.

You Need:
- red or white pipe cleaners
- red and white tri-beads

Candy Cane Ornaments

1. Alternate red and white beads on the pipe cleaner covering it completely.

2. Twist and bend the ends of the pipe cleaner to form knots to keep the beads in place.

3. Bend the beaded pipe cleaner in the shape of a candy cane.

Golden Gifts

You Need:
- tag board
- ribbon
- gold spray paint
- margarine lids
- paper punch
- glue
- scissors
- variety of macaroni shapes

1. Trace a margarine lid and cut out a circle from tagboard.

2. Punch a hole at the top of the circle.

3. Glue on a variety of macaroni noodles covering the circle completely.

4. Take the ball to a well ventilated area and spray it with gold paint.

5. When dry, loop the ribbon through the hole and give the ornament as a gift.

You Need:
- white lunch bags
- red pompoms
- red construction paper
- wiggle eyes
- cotton balls
- glue

Santa Gift Bags

1. Fold over the top one third of the bag to make a triangle.

2. Cut a red construction paper triangle to fit on the bag's triangle and glue it down to make Santa's hat.

3. Glue a cotton ball to the tip of the hat.

4. Glue two eyes in the center of the bag.

5. Glue on the pompom for the nose.

6. Pull apart and glue cotton balls to make Santa's beard.

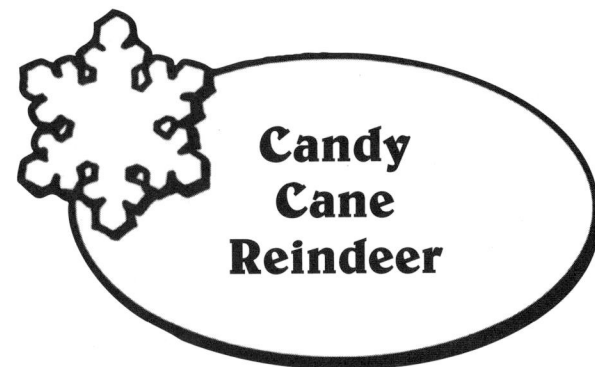

Candy Cane Reindeer

You Need:
- candy canes
- brown pipe cleaners
- self-stick wiggle eyes
- mini red pompoms

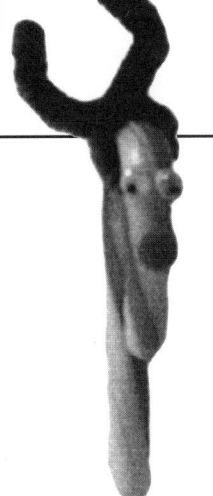

1. Unwrap the candy cane.

2. Twist a pipe cleaner around the curve of the candy cane to form antlers.

3. Stick on eyes.

4. Glue on the pompom for the nose.

You Need:
- red or green felt
- red or green ribbon, 1/8" wide
- paper punch
- self adhesive Velcro
- small silver bells, 5 for each student

Jingle Bell Bracelets

Before the Party:
- Cut 1" wide strips of felt long enough to fit around students' wrists or ankles.
- Cut ribbon into 3" lengths.

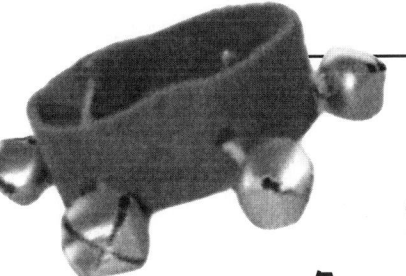

1. Attach Velcro to each end of the felt strip so it will clasp together.

2. Punch 5 holes around the felt bracelet.

3. Thread ribbon through each bell and attach them to the bracelet by threading them through each hole in the bracelet.

4. Clasp the bracelet around the wrist or ankle.

Marshmallow Magic

You Need:
- mini marshmallows
- toothpicks
- white ribbon
- hot glue gun

1. Create snowflakes with marshmallows by grouping them together using toothpicks.

2. Hot glue a ribbon under one of the marshmallows for hanging.

You Need:
- pictures of each student's face
- snowman tracers
- white fun foam
- paper punch
- black construction paper
- tape
- glue
- ribbon
- buttons
- cloth ribbon
- small sticks

Picture Perfect Snowmen

Before the Party:
- Duplicate the snowman on page 123 and make several tracers out of tagboard.

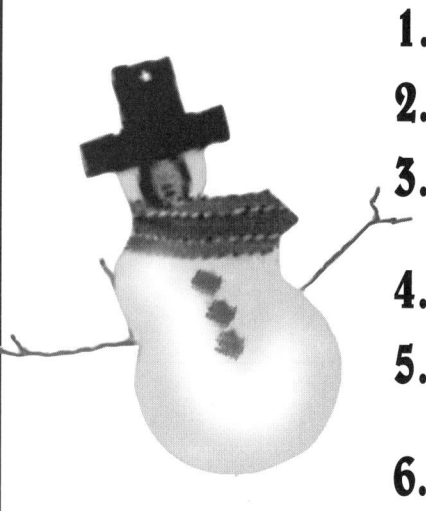

1. Trace and cut a snowman from the fun foam.

2. Glue a picture on the head portion of the snowman.

3. Decorate by gluing on buttons and tying a cloth ribbon scarf around the neck.

4. Tape sticks to the back of the snowman to form arms.

5. Make a top hat with black construction paper and glue on the snowman's head.

6. Punch a hole in the top hat.

7. Loop a ribbon through the hole and tie to hang.

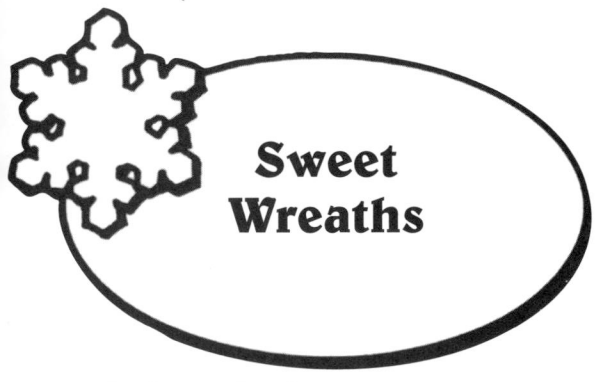

Sweet Wreaths

You Need:
- sturdy wire
- lifesavers
- popped popcorn
- gumdrops
- mini marshmallows
- cranberries
- donut-shaped cereal
- holiday ribbon

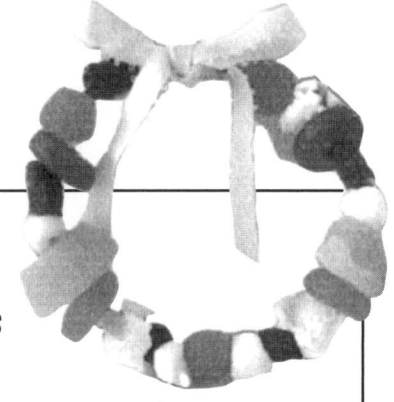

Before the Party:
- Cut wire into 14" lengths.

1. String food on the wire.

2. Bend the wire into a wreath shape and twist the ends together.

3. Tie a bow around the twisted ends.

You Need:
- 12" x 18" brown, white, and black construction paper
- red poms
- scissors
- stapler
- pencils

Rudolph at the Head

Before the Party:
- Cut brown paper into 3" x 18" strips.

1. Staple the brown strips together to make a headband for each student.

2. Trace and cut two hands out of brown paper.

3. Staple the hands to the inside of the headband to form antlers.

4. Make eyes using black and white paper and glue them to the front of the headband.

5. Add a red pom for a nose and wear the party hat!

Holiday Stationary

You Need:
- white paper
- white envelopes
- stamps
- stamp pads
- holiday ribbon

1. Using the stamps, decorate sheets of paper and the envelopes to match.

2. Bundle them together with the ribbon and tie in a bow.

Sugar and Spice

You Need:
- applesauce
- rolling pin
- waxed paper
- bowl
- ground cinnamon
- holiday cookie cutters
- holiday ribbon
- pencils

Before the Party:
- Cut ribbon into 20" lengths.

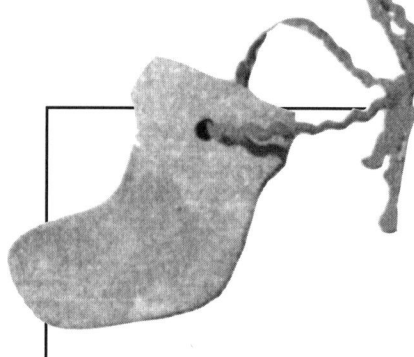

1. Mix 1/4 cup applesauce and 1 oz. cinnamon in a bowl.

2. Form the mixture into a ball.

3. On waxed paper, roll the dough to 1/4" thick with the rolling pin.

4. Use a cookie cutter to cut out a shape.

5. Using a pencil eraser, punch a hole in the top of the dough shape.

6. Set aside to dry.

7. String and tie a holiday ribbon through the hole to hang.

Stitched Stockings

You Need:
- stocking tracers
- tag board
- felt
- scissors
- hot glue gun
- embroidery needle and thread

Before the Party:
- Make stocking tracers from tag board using the pattern on page 124.

1. Trace the stocking pattern on two pieces of felt.

2. Cut out the stockings.

3. Glue around the edges of one stocking leaving the top of the stocking free from glue.

4. Place the second stocking over the first to glue together.

5. Decorate the stockings by sewing around the edges with the embroidery needle and thread.

You Need:
- dull tapestry needles
- fishing line
- cranberries
- mini marshmallows
- lifesavers
- beads
- bowls
- dry cereal
- buttons
- macaroni noodles
- popped popcorn

Garland Galore

1. Thread a needle and knot the end of the thread around the first item chosen to string on the garland.

2. String the garland as desired.

3. Knot the end of the string around the last item on the garland.

Cool Bookmarks

You Need:
- blue tag board
- clear contact paper
- white snowflake sequins
- ribbon
- scissors
- glue
- silver gel pens
- paper punch

Before the Party:
- Cut tag board into 3" x 6" rectangles to make bookmarks.
- Cut contact paper into 4" x 7" rectangles.

1. Write students' names on each bookmark using the gel pen.

2. Glue on sequins.

3. Cover the bookmark with the contact paper.

4. Punch a hole at the top of the bookmark and tie a ribbon through the hole.

You Need:
- ruler
- scissors
- permanent marker
- polar fleece fabric

Winter Wraps

Before the Party:
- Cut the fleece into 1 yard by 8 inch pieces. One for each student. (A fabric store may do this for you.)

1. Using marker, students draw a vertical line 6 inches from each end of their fabric.

2. Beginning at each end of the fabric, cut strips approximately 8 inches apart up to the marked line.

3. Make tassels by tying a knot at the end of each fabric strip.

Juggling Snowballs

You Need:
- white balloons, 3 per child
- rice
- funnel

1. Inflate and deflate the balloons several times to stretch them out.

2. Place the funnel into the balloon opening.

3. Fill the balloon 2/3 full of rice.

4. Knot the balloon and push the knot into the balloon.

5. Find some space and practice juggling!

You Need:
- toilet paper rolls
- rubber bands
- small, hard candy
- wrapping paper
- curling ribbon
- waxed paper
- trinkets
- stickers
- tape

Party Poppers

Before the Party:
- Cut two 4" circle shapes out of waxed paper.
- Cut wrapping paper in 6" x 11" pieces.

1. Place one waxed paper circle over the end of a toilet paper roll and secure it with a rubber band.

2. Fill the tube with candy, stickers, and trinkets.

3. Place a waxed paper circle on the other end of the roll and secure it with a rubber band.

4. Roll the wrapping paper around the tube and tape it to hold together.

5. Twist the ends of the wrapping paper and tie them with curling ribbon.

Stick to Snowmen

You Need:
- white spray paint
- black fun foam
- wiggle eyes
- cloth ribbon
- magnetic adhesive strips
- paint stir sticks
- glue
- buttons
- felt-tip markers

Before the Party:
- Spray paint the stir sticks white.
- Cut the magnetic adhesive into 1" strips.
- Cut ribbon into 6 inch lengths.

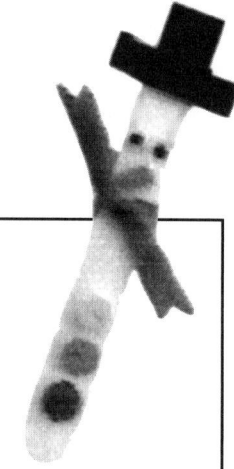

1. Cut out a hat from the fun foam and glue it on top of the paint stick.

2. Decorate with the other materials to make a snowman.

3. Stick the magnetic strip to the back of the snowman.

You Need:
- pine cones
- peanut butter
- plastic knives
- ribbon
- bird seed
- paper plates

It's for the Birds

Before the Party:
- Tie a ribbon around the top of each pine cone.

1. Spread peanut butter over the entire pine cone.

2. Shake bird seed on a plate and roll the pine cone in the bird seed.

3. Shake off any loose seeds.

Winter Treats

For ease and neatness we suggest students prepare their party treats on paper plates.

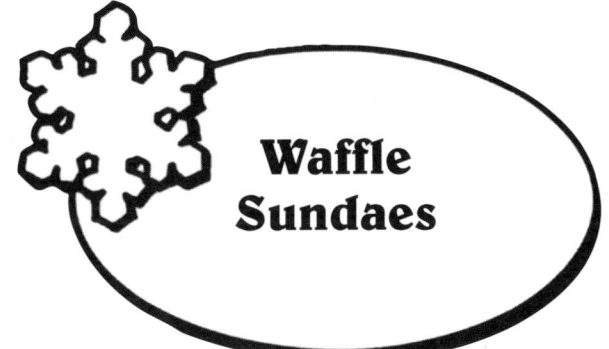

Waffle Sundaes

You Need:
- frozen waffles
- ice cream toppings
- sturdy paper plates
- candy canes
- ice cream
- toaster
- spoons

1. Lightly toast a waffle.

2. Place a scoop of ice cream on top of the waffle.

3. Add toppings of your choice including a candy cane.

Ice Fishing Feasts

You Need:
- dowels, one for every two students
- 2' strings, one per child
- powdered sugar mini donuts
- large plastic bags

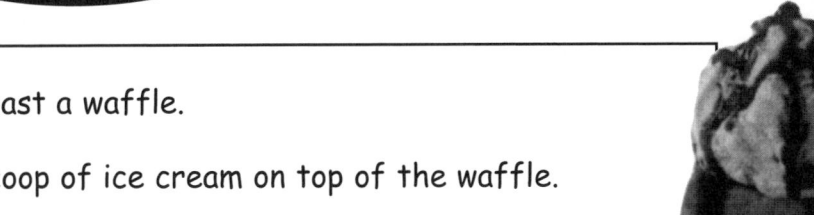

Before the Party:
- Tie a string around each donut and store it in a plastic bag.

1. Tie the empty end of the donut string to a dowel.

2. One student is fishing and another is the fish. The fish lies down on their back with their head at the feet of the student fishing.

3. The student who's fishing feeds the donut bait to the fish.

4. The fish must lie still and use only their mouth to eat the bait.

5. When finished, the students switch places using a new string and donut bait.

Snowflake Fiesta

You Need:
- flour tortillas
- easy squirt cheese

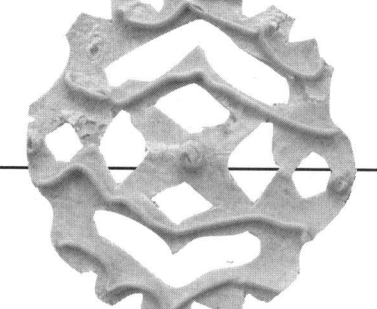

1. Fold a tortilla in half, then in half again.

2. Bite the tortilla to form a snowflake.

3. Unfold the snowflake and add cheese before eating.

Crispy Treats

You Need:
- rice cereal bars
- assorted candy
- tongue depressors
- green frosting
- plastic knives

1. Flatten the rice cereal bar with your hand.

2. Cut out a tree shape using the plastic knife.

3. Push the tongue depressor into the tree bar.

4. Spread the tree with green frosting.

5. Decorate with candy.

Graham Cracker Gifts

You Need:
- graham crackers, 2 per student
- green frosting
- red shoestring licorice
- peanut butter
- knives

1. Spread peanut butter on one graham cracker and top with another cracker.

2. Spread frosting over both crackers.

3. Tie the crackers together with the licorice making a ribbon and bow.

Tree Treats

You Need:
- sugar cones
- gumdrops
- small chocolate candies
- green mint ice cream
- plastic spoons & knives
- green frosting
- red hots
- plastic bowls
- red licorice strings
- small paper plates

1. Place a sugar cone upside down on a paper plate.

2. Spread the frosting completely covering the cone.

3. Decorate with candy.

4. Place a scoop of ice cream in a bowl and put the cone on top.

Candy Cane Sundaes

You Need:
- vanilla ice cream
- ice cream toppings
- plastic bowls
- metal and plastic spoons
- mini candy canes
- whipped cream
- plastic zipper bags

1. Place two candy canes in a plastic bag.

2. Crush the candy canes using the back of a metal spoon.

3. Scoop ice cream in a bowl and sprinkle with crushed candy.

4. Add toppings of your choice.

Popping Snowflakes

You Need:
- air popper
- popcorn
- clean, flat sheet

1. Place the popper on a sheet in the center of the room.

2. Take off the air popper lid and add popcorn.

3. Students stand OFF the sheet.

4. Watch the popcorn pop around the room.

5. Enjoy eating it when it's finished!

You Need:
- chocolate sandwich cookies
- mini twist pretzels
- raisins
- plastic knives
- red hots
- white frosting

Raisin Rudolphs

Before the Party:
- Cut large squares of waxed paper.

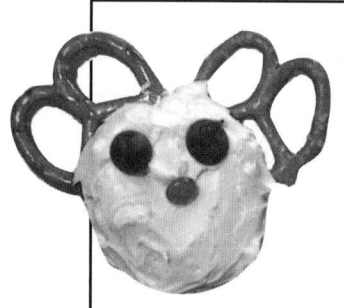

1. Frost a cookie with the frosting so it is completely covered.

2. Press the pretzels to the frosting to form antlers.

3. Place two raisins to form eyes and one red hot for Rudolph's nose.

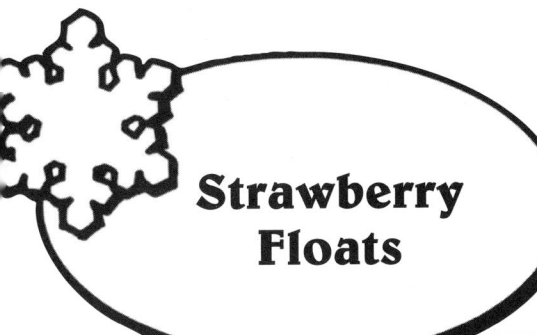

Strawberry Floats

You Need:
- vanilla ice cream
- candy canes
- spoons
- straws
- strawberry pop
- large plastic cups

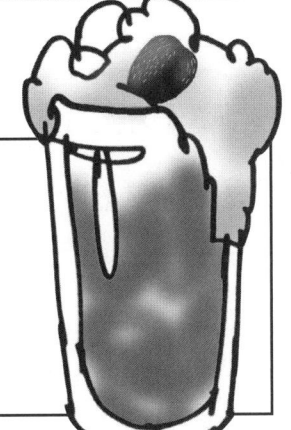

1. Put two scoops of ice cream in a cup.

2. Pour strawberry pop over the ice cream.

3. Add a straw, spoon, and candy cane to serve.

You Need:
- graham crackers
- chocolate bars
- large marshmallows

Scrumptious S'mores

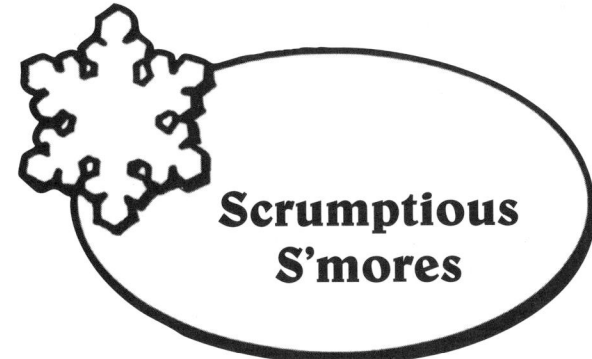

1. Build a s'more by placing a marshmallow and chocolate bar between two graham crackers.

2. Microwave (if possible) for 15 seconds.

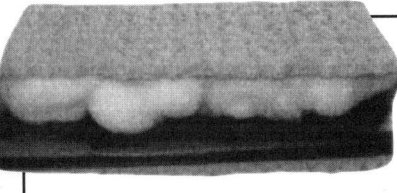

Shiver Me Warm

You Need:
- peppermint ice cream
- chocolate milk
- peppermint sticks
- mugs
- crock pot
- spoons

1. Heat milk in a crock pot.

2. Serve milk in a mug with a scoop of peppermint ice cream, a peppermint "stir" stick, and a spoon.

Valentine Mixers

A mixer is the kick-off activity to the party. It involves the entire class, building excitement for the party and setting the stage for fun.

Heart to Heart

You Need:
- candy conversation hearts
- bowl

1. Sit in a circle.

2. Pass the bowl of candy around the circle and each student takes one heart.

3. One student begins a story by saying a sentence that uses the word(s) on their heart.

4. Continue around the circle and have each child add to the story by saying a sentence that uses the word(s) on their candy heart.

You Need:
- 12 chairs
- CD or cassette player
- love songs

Love Seat

1. Set up a circle of chairs that are facing outward.

2. Stand outside the circle.

3. Begin the music and students walk around the chairs.

4. When the music stops everyone finds a chair to sit in, or if a chair is not available, students sit on the laps of other students.

5. Continue playing by taking away one chair each time until all the students are piled on 4 or 5 chairs.

Perfect Pairs

You Need:
- index cards

Before the Party:
- Choosing from the list below, write each word on an index card.

1. Each student receives one index card.

2. Students move around the room looking for a card that will pair with the word on their index card.

3. When everyone has found their partner, form a circle and share the perfect pairs.

Suggested Word Pairs

ketchup & mustard
green eggs & ham
m & m's
Beauty & the Beast
hamburger & fries
salt & pepper

pail & shovel
Jack & Jill
milk & cookies
Snow White & 7 Dwarfs
macaroni & cheese
Mickey Mouse & Minnie Mouse

hugs & kisses
peanut butter & jelly
hat & mittens
soap & water
paper & pencil

You Need:
- red sock
- kitchen timer with a loud ticking sound

The Beating Heart

1. Two or three students leave the classroom.

2. Choose a place to hide the timer, then set it for 2 minutes. Place the timer in the sock and hide the "beating heart."

3. Usher the students back in the room and explain that they need to find the heart before it quits beating.

4. Repeat the game as many times as desired.

Topsy Turvy Hearts

You Need:
◆ two heart-shaped balloons

Before the Party:
• Blow up the balloons.

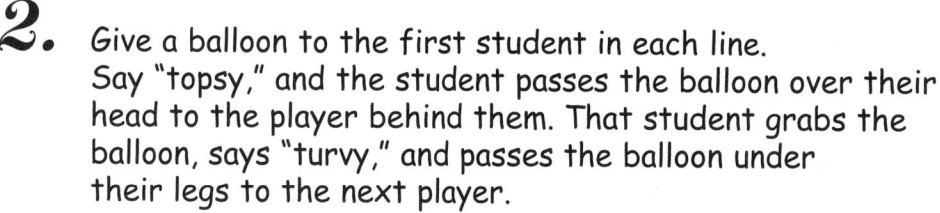

1. Divide the class into 2 groups and each group line up in single file.

2. Give a balloon to the first student in each line. Say "topsy," and the student passes the balloon over their head to the player behind them. That student grabs the balloon, says "turvy," and passes the balloon under their legs to the next player.

3. Continue with each child saying "topsy" or "turvy" as they pass the balloon. The last player in line runs with the balloon to the front of the line and play begins again.

4. When the original player is first in line again, the team sits down.

Shaping Up

1. Working together as an entire class, students form one large heart using their bodies.

2. If possible, take a picture from above the class heart.

Straight as an Arrow

1. Divide the class into two teams.

2. Shout out a direction as to how the teams should line up. The two teams put themselves in that order, as straight as an arrow, and as quickly as they can.

Suggested directions: *birthdates, beginning with January*
tallest to shortest
whoever is wearing the most/least amount of red
alphabetical order of first names

<u>You Need:</u>
◆   red and purple washable markers

Fancy Footwork

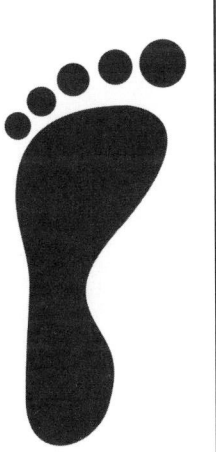 

1. Divide the class into two groups.

2. Students remove their right socks and shoes.

3. An adult writes in marker a letter from a Valentine saying on each student's foot. Both groups will have the same phrase written on their feet but with a different marker color.

4. The two groups perform some fancy footwork and see who is the first to unscramble the Valentine phrase by lining their feet up in the correct order.

Suggested phrases: *Hugs and Kisses*
Be my Valentine
You are sweet
Bee my honey

Standing Still

You Need:
- index cards, 1 per student
- pencils
- large bowl

Before the Party:
- Number each index card 1,2,3 on one side and 4,5,6 on the other side, leaving space for the students to write answers by each number.

1. Give each student an index card and pencil.

2. Ask six questions, one at a time to the class. Suggested questions:

Are you excited for the Valentine party?
What is your favorite animal?
What is your mom's first name?
What is your teacher's last name?
What is your favorite food?
What are your initials?

3. Students write their answers on the cards.

4. Collect the cards and put them in a bowl.

5. Sit in a circle.

6. This mixer will be played two times using 3 questions for each game. An adult chooses one card from the bowl and asks the first question then reads the answer from the card that was chosen. Any student who answered the question the same as the card read, stands up.

7. Now ask only the students standing the second question and read the next answer from the card. Those students that answered question number two the same as what was read from the card remain standing. All others sit.

8. Continue with the third question and answer. The student whose card was chosen should be the only student yet standing at the end of all three questions.

9. Repeat the game using another answer card for questions 4,5,6.

Valentine Trivia

1. Students sit in a circle.

2. An adult reads trivia statements to the class.

3. Students who think the answer is true, stand up.
   Students who believe the answer to be false, remain seated.

Mother's Day falls on February 14. (false - Valentine's Day)

A rose is a flower that represents love and is the most popular flower given on Valentine's Day. (true)

Cupid is the god of joy who was worshiped by ancient Romans. (false - god of love)

Cupid carried a bow and shot arrows that had silver tips. (false - gold tips)

Legend said anyone struck by Cupid's arrows fell instantly in love. (true)

A Valentine heart symbolizes love, but the heart in your body is a hard working muscle. (true)

Valentine's Day is named after a priest named Valentine who was put to death on February 13. (false - February 14)

Valentine's Day is a popular day to get married. (true)

The biggest Hershey's kiss ever made was 200 pounds. (false - 400 pounds)

Almost 7 billion candy hearts are sold each Valentine's Day. (true)

Principals receive the most Valentine cards. (false - teachers)

Lovebirds are colorful birds with red beaks and live in France. (false - Africa)

Valentine Team Builders

These team builders are designed to form four groups of students.
Make quantity adjustments according to the number of students in your class.

Bubble Blast

You Need:
- wrapped bubble gum in four different colors
- decorated bag

1. Place the gum in the bag.

2. Each student takes one piece of gum, unwraps it, and begins to chew. Chew for several minutes to soften the gum.

3. Say "blow," and students blow a bubble and hold it.

4. Match bubbles of the same color to form groups.

You Need:
- 1 red, pink, purple, and white piece of 9" x 12" construction paper
- large bowl

Broken Hearts

Before the Party:
- Cut a large heart out of each color of construction paper.
- Cut the hearts into as many puzzle pieces that are required to form each group.
- Put all the puzzle pieces in a large bowl.

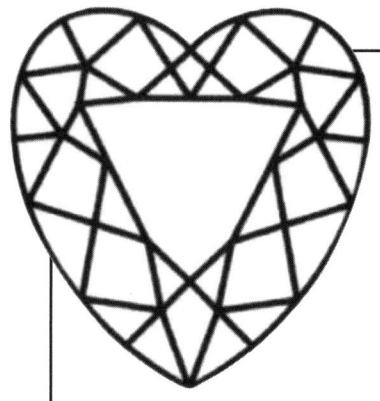

1. Each student picks one puzzle piece from the bowl.

2. Say "go," and students form groups by finding other students with puzzle pieces of the same color.

3. The groups then piece their broken hearts back together.

Hearts in Harmony

You Need:
- white, purple, red, and pink construction paper
- love songs
- CD or cassette player

Before the Party:
- Cut an equal number of hearts from each color of paper, 1 heart per student.

1. Stand in a circle

2. Give everyone a heart to hold.

3. As the music begins playing, students pass the heart to the player next to them. Continue passing until the music stops.

4. Students form groups by finding others who are holding the same colored heart.

You Need:
- small balloons, 1 per child
- red, pink, purple, and white copy paper

Balloon Burst

Before the Party:
- Cut an equal number of small hearts from each color of paper.
- Roll up the hearts and put one inside each balloon.
- Blow up and tie the balloons. Place them around the room.

1. Each student chooses a balloon from around the room.

2. Students form one large circle.

3. Say "pop," and students sit on their balloons and pop them.

4. Students form groups with others who have the same colored hearts in their balloons.

Valentine Games

These games have been designed to play with small groups of students.

Marshmallow Mumble

You Need:
- large marshmallows
- paper
- garbage bags

<u>Before the Party:</u>
- Write valentine sayings on slips of paper.
  Suggested sayings: *I love you.*
                       Hug me.
                       Kiss me.
                       Be my valentine.

1. One student at a time chooses a slip of paper, stuffs 3-5 marshmallows in their mouth, and reads aloud the saying on the paper.

2. Other students try to guess what is being said.

3. When finished, spit the marshmallows out in the garbage.

Tissue Toot

You Need:
- party blowers, one per student
- facial tissues

1. Students pair up. One child lays on the ground, the other kneels at their head.

2. The child on the ground places a tissue over their mouth and nose and blows the tissue up in the air.

3. The child who is kneeling blows their horn and tries to catch the tissue with the horn.

4. Students switch places, each using a new horn and tissue.

Wheelbarrow Race

You Need:
- small paper plates
- small unwrapped candy, such as candy coated chocolate pieces

1. Students pair up.

2. Partners wheelbarrow down to a plate of four candies. The player on the floor eats the candy using only their mouth.

3. Partners wheelbarrow back to the beginning and switch positions. A new plate with candy is put down for the next person.

You Need:
- maze
- magazines
- pencils

Magazine Maze

Before the Party:
- Reproduce the maze on page 125 for each student.

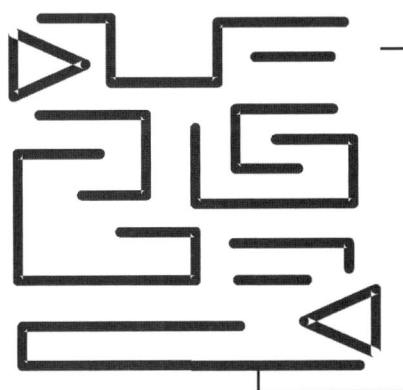

1. Students make their way through the maze by finding items in a magazine that are listed on the maze.

2. Students write the page number of each item found.

Meet Me in the Middle

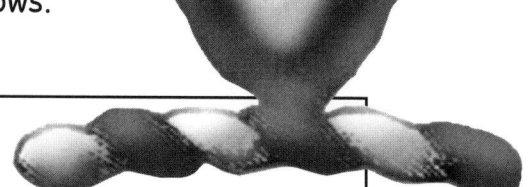

You Need:
- red shoestring licorice
- large marshmallows

Before the Party:
- Poke a hole in the middle of the marshmallows and thread one piece of licorice through two marshmallows.

1. Students divide into pairs and face each other.

2. Partners each hold an end of the licorice string making sure the marshmallows are hanging in the middle.

3. Say "chew," and students eat their half of the licorice and try to be the first to reach the marshmallows.

You Need:
- 9" x 12" red or pink construction paper
- CD or cassette player

Have a Heart

Before the Party:
- Cut out large hearts.
- Set the hearts in a circle, one less than the number of students playing.

1. Stand in a circle outside the hearts.

2. When the music begins, students march, glide, hop, or skip around the circle.

3. When the music stops, students must find a heart to stand on. Those that don't have a heart find a heart to share with a friend.

4. Remove one heart each time you play until everyone is sharing one heart.

Red-y for Charades

Before the Party:
- Write words of things that are red on slips of paper.
  Suggested words:

stop sign	rose
Rudolph's nose	firetruck
fire hydrant	apple
heart	Santa
Clifford	exit sign
bullfighter's cape	candy cane

1. Tell the students they will be acting out and guessing items that are red.

2. Students choose a slip of paper and act out the word.

Balloon Bounce

You Need:
- red, pink, white and purple balloons, 1 per student
- chopsticks, 1 set per student

Before the Party:
- Blow up the balloons.

1. Each student receives a balloon and a pair of chopsticks.

2. Say "bounce," and students bat their balloon with the chopsticks trying to keep it from touching the ground.

3. Students sit down if their balloon touches the ground.

4. Play continues until one student is left standing.

Winter Golf

You Need:
- stale, hard marshmallows
- plastic golf clubs

Before the Party:

- Set up a golf course throughout the room by placing objects on the ground to designate fairways. You don't need to set up greens or holes.

  Suggested objects: *chair legs   overturned cups   rulers or yardsticks*
  book tunnel   tagboard ramps   pencils

1. Each student takes a turn putting a marshmallow through the golf course. Count the number of strokes it takes to get through the course.

You Need:
- recognizable objects, such as a pencil, scissors, paper clip, safety pin, fork, or saw
- red spray paint   •   pencils
- paper   •   white construction paper

I See Red

Before the Party:

- Place one object at a time on a single piece of white paper and spray the object and paper red.
- Remove the object so a silhouette appears.
- Number each silhouette.

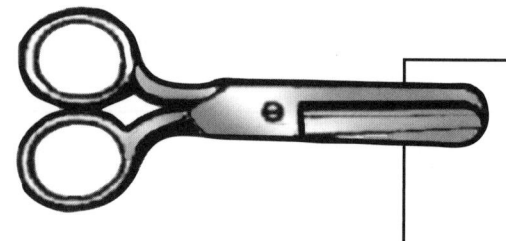

1. Give each student a paper and pencil.

2. Students look at each silhouette, try to guess what it is, and write an answer on their paper next to the corresponding number of the object.

Hop To It

You Need:
- dice
- masking tape

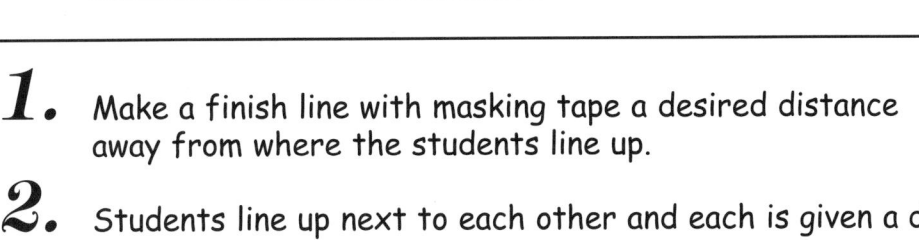

1. Make a finish line with masking tape a desired distance away from where the students line up.

2. Students line up next to each other and each is given a die.

3. Say "hop," and students roll the dice at their feet.
They pick up the dice and hop as many times toward the finish line as the number rolled.
If a 1 is rolled, players go back to start.
If a 3 is rolled, players hop backwards 3 hops.

4. Continue playing until players hop across the finish line.

Hot Air Balloon Blow

You Need:
- heart balloons, 1 per student

Before the Party:
- Blow up the balloons.

1. Each student is given one balloon and lines up on their hands and knees behind a start line.

2. Say "blow," and students blow their balloon to a turn around line, pick up the balloon, and run back to start.

Gumdrop Chop

You Need:
- ◆ chopsticks, 1 set per student
- ◆ 2 small paper cups per student
- ◆ red gumdrops

Before the Party:
- • Count 15 gumdrops into a cup for each student.

1. Give each student a cup of gumdrops, a pair of chopsticks, and an empty cup.

2. Say "chop to it," and the students use chopsticks to pick up 1 gumdrop at a time and drop it in their empty cups. The gumdrops that make it to the empty cups without being dropped on the ground can be eaten.

You Need:
- ◆ pink and red balloons   ◆ paper plates
- ◆ red, white & pink tissue paper
- ◆ markers

It's Electrifying

Before the Party:
- • Cut the tissue paper into 2" hearts.
- • Blow up the balloons.

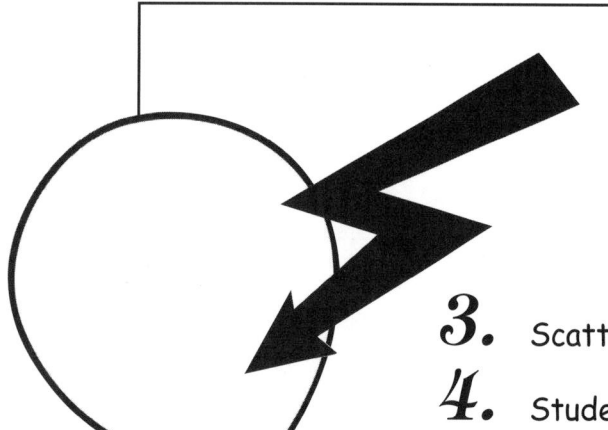

1. Give each student a paper plate and have them write their name in large letters on the front.

2. Students form a circle and set their paper plates behind them.

3. Scatter the hearts in the middle of the circle.

4. Students rub the balloons on their hair to create static electricity. For 3 minutes students pick up hearts on the balloons and put them on their paper plates. At the end of the time period students count the number of hearts they collected.

Pretzel Puzzle

1. Select one student to be the pretzel puzzle solver and ask him/her to leave the room.

2. The remaining students hold hands and twist and tangle themselves into one gigantic pretzel.

3. The puzzle solver returns to the room and tries to direct the students to untangle themselves.

4. Repeat the activity with a new pretzel puzzle solver.

Spoonful of Sugar

You Need:
* 4 bowls   * 2 spoons   * candy hearts

1. Divide the students into 2 groups and line them up in 2 lines.

2. Place bowls filled with candy hearts next to each group.

3. Place 2 empty bowls across the room.

4. Say "scoop," and the first person in each line takes a spoon and scoops up as many hearts that fit on the spoon.

5. Students walk to the empty bowl, pour the candy into the bowl, and race back to the next person in line.

6. Candy that falls may not be picked up.

7. After all have played, count the candy hearts in each team's bowl.

A Valentine Twist

You Need:
- ◆ 1 white flat sheet
- ◆ 2 bowls
- ◆ index cards
- ◆ red, pink, and purple fabric paint
- ◆ red, pink, and purple paper

Before the Party:
- • Paint 12 large hearts on the sheet, 4 of each color, red, pink, and purple.
- • Cut out 8 red, pink, and purple hearts.
- • Write body parts on index cards.
  Suggested body parts:

right foot	left foot
elbow	knee
right hand	left hand

1. Place the paper hearts in one bowl and the index cards in another bowl.

2. Students stand on the outside edge of the sheet. Choose a leader to be the caller.

3. The leader picks a colored heart from one bowl and a body part from the other. The first player must place that body part on the matching colored heart on the sheet.

4. The leader draws another body part and heart for the next student. Continue playing until someone falls.

You Need:
- ◆ 25 heart-shaped stickers per student
- ◆ dice

On a Roll

Before the Party:
- • Reproduce the grid on page 126 for each student.

1. Students take turns rolling the die and placing that number of stickers on their grid.

2. Continue playing until everyone fills their grid.

Take the Cake

You Need:
- cupcakes
- bowl
- CD or cassette player
- 12 index cards

Before the Party:
- Write the numbers 1 - 6 on two sets of index cards.

1. An adult tapes one set of numbers around a table and places a cupcake at each spot. The other set of numbers are put in a bowl.

2. When the music begins students march around the table.

3. When the music stops students stand by a number.

4. The adult picks a number out of the bowl.

5. The student standing next to that number keeps the cupcake.

6. Continue playing until everyone has won a cupcake.

Sweetie Pie

You Need:
- aluminum foil
- bubble gum
- pie plate, 1 per student
- spray container of whipped topping

1. Give each student a piece of bubble gum and a pie plate.

2. Students remove the wrapper from their gum and place the gum in the pie plate.

3. Squirt whipped topping so it completely covers the pie tin.

4. Say "sweetie pie," and students use only their mouths to find their gum, chew it up, and blow big bubbles.

Valentine Crafts

Quantities should be determined by the number of students at each station.

Seeds of Love

You Need:
- small clay pots
- potting soil
- craft sticks
- permanent markers
- reclosable sandwich bags
- flower and heart-shaped stickers
- spoons
- flower seeds
- glue
- construction paper

1. Decorate a pot using stickers and/or markers.

2. Scoop soil into the plastic bag and add several seeds.

3. Place a bag of soil into the pot.

4. Glue the flower to the craft stick and place it behind the bag of soil.

5. Plant the seeds at home in the flower pot.

FANtastic Fun

You Need:
- gift wrap
- markers
- stapler
- construction paper
- white copy paper
- glue

Before the Party:
- Cut gift wrap into 8 1/2" X 11" pieces.

1. Fold a piece of gift wrap into a fan and staple one end together.

2. Write the message *You are FANtastic!* on the white paper and glue it on the construction paper.

3. Glue the edges of the fan to the construction paper.

4. Decorate the rest of the valentine card.

Light Up Your Life

You Need:
- baby food jars
- glue
- bowls
- red, pink, and white tissue paper
- paint brushes
- tea light candles
- spoons

Before the Party:
- Cut tissue paper into 1" squares.

1. Thin the glue with a few drops of water.

2. Paint the glue on a jar.

3. Cover the jar with overlapping tissue paper squares. Add glue where necessary.

4. Place a tea light inside the jar.

You Need:
- red and black felt
- glue
- uncooked rice
- hot glue gun
- small paper cup
- wiggle eyes

Lovely Ladybugs

Before the Party:
For each child...
- Cut 2, red 4" ovals.
- Cut 1, 3 1/2" x 1/2" black felt strips.
- Cut 1, 1 1/2" black semi-circle.
- Cut 4, 1" black felt circles.
- Cut 1, 4" x 1/2" black felt strips.

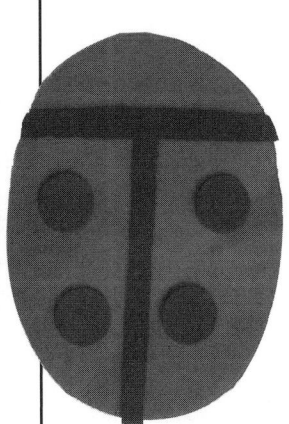

1. Glue a black strip down the center of one red oval.

2. Glue the remaining black strip to form a "T."

3. Glue 2 black felt spots on each side of the "T."

4. Hot glue the 2 red ovals together leaving an opening at the top.

5. Using the small cup, pour rice into the bug's body.

6. Hot glue the opening.

7. Glue the semi circle to the top of the body to make the ladybug's head.

8. Add wiggle eyes if desired.

I Love Ewe

You Need:
- scissors
- cotton balls
- wiggle eyes
- 8 1/2" x 11" black construction paper
- white crayons
- glue

1. Fold the construction paper in half.

2. Place one hand on the paper laying the wrist on the folded edge. Spread out the fingers and trace the hand.

3. Cut out without cutting on the fold.

4. Turn the hand so the fingers are facing down making the legs of a sheep.

5. Glue an eye on the thumb and cotton balls on the hand to make the sheep's wool.

6. Open the card and write "I LOVE EWE!" using a white crayon.

Beary Sweet

You Need:
- brown or white plastic spoons
- wiggle eyes
- mini black pom poms
- valentine ribbon
- glue
- round suckers
- brown poms

Before the Party:
- Cut ribbon into 12" lengths.

1. Glue 2 brown poms high on the back side of the spoon to make ears.

2. Glue two eyes and a black pom nose below the ears.

3. Place a sucker on the inside of the spoon and tie the sucker and spoon together with a ribbon.

Friendship Bracelets

Before the Party:
- Cut the thread into 12" lengths.

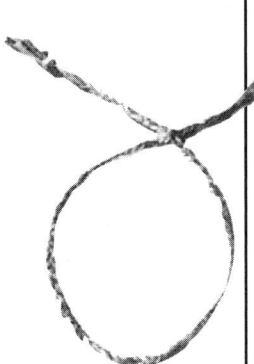

1. Tie and knot 3 strands of thread together at one end.

2. One friend holds the knot while the other braids the strands together.

3. Knot the thread together at the end of the braid.

4. Tie the bracelet around an ankle or wrist.

5. Switch roles so the other friend makes a bracelet.

Catchy Caterpillars

You Need:
- assorted colored poms
- magnetic strips
- wooden clip clothespins
- 8 1/2" by 11" red, white, and pink paper
- small wiggle eyes
- glue
- pipe cleaners

Before the Party:
- Cut pipe cleaners into 4" lengths.
- Cut construction paper into fourths.

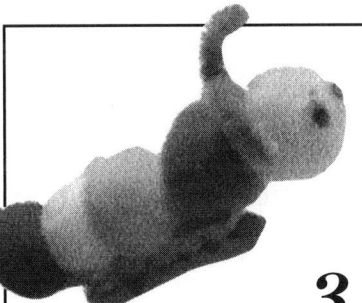

1. Glue poms on the flat side of the clothespin to form the caterpillar's body.

2. Glue 2 eyes on the pom that covers the clothespin's clip.

3. To form the antennae, twist the pipe cleaner between the first and second pom.

4. Place a magnetic strip on the backside of the clothespin.

5. Cut hearts out of paper.

6. Use the clothespin to clip and hold the hearts together.

7. Place it on the refrigerator and use hearts for love notes.

Royal Goblets

You Need:
- plastic wine glasses
- soft pink or white modeling clay
- fake gems and beads

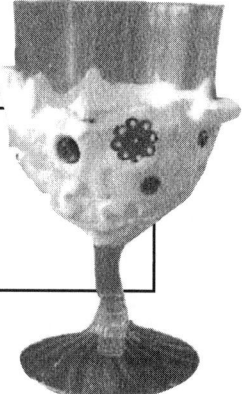

1. Press the clay around the base and bottom half of the glass.

2. Press the gems and beads into the clay.

Nummy Necklaces

You Need:
- red or pink plastic wrap or cellophane
- variety of wrapped valentine candy
- curling ribbon

Before the Party:
- Cut the ribbon into 7" lengths, 6 - 8 strands per necklace.

1. Give each student 3 feet of plastic wrap.

2. Lay the wrap flat and fold it lengthwise.

3. Place candy every 3 inches on the strip.

4. Roll up the plastic wrap and candy.

5. Tie ribbon between each candy piece and one ribbon at each end.

6. Use the end ribbons to tie the necklace around the students' necks.

Keepsake Quotes

You Need:
- proverbs
- red pencils
- pink or red curling ribbon

Before the Party:
- Reproduce the proverbs on page 127.
- Cut the curling ribbon into 12" lengths.

1. An adult reads each proverb to the student.

2. Students use a red pencil to fill in the blank with an answer they think makes sense.

3. Roll up the paper similar to a scroll and tie it with ribbon to give as a gift.

Smooch the Pooch

You Need:
- white or brown paper lunch bag
- scissors
- paper punch
- purple, white, pink, red, and blue construction paper
- glue
- yarn

1. Cut an assortment of heart shapes from different colors of paper.

2. Glue two large hearts on top of the bag for ears.

3. Glue smaller hearts for eyes and nose.

4. To form the mouth, glue a heart upside down on the fold of the bag. Add a small heart for the tongue.

5. Glue a variety of hearts on the bag to make spots.

6. Make a bone for the dog's name tag. Punch a hole on both ends of the bone and thread the yarn through to make a collar. Tape the ribbon ends to the back of the bag.

Love Sachets

You Need:

- valentine fabric
- measuring cup
- bowl
- spoons
- potpourri
- rubber bands
- lace
- thin valentine ribbon

Before the Party:

For each child...

- Cut 8" circles from the fabric.
- Cut 10" circles from the lace.
- Cut ribbon into 10" lengths.

1. Lay the fabric flat, print side down.

2. Scoop 1/2 cup potpourri and pour it in the center of the fabric.

3. Gather the fabric around the potpourri and secure it with a rubber band.

4. Place the sachet in the center of the lace. Gather the lace around the sachet and tie it together with ribbon.

You Need:

- 8 1/2" x 11" red construction paper
- envelopes
- markers
- valentine stickers

Card Cut Ups

1. Cut a large heart from the paper.

2. In large letters, write a valentine message to someone special and decorate the heart.

3. Cut the heart into 6 - 8 pieces.

4. Place the puzzle pieces in an envelope.

5. Address the envelope and decorate it with stickers.

Fun Foam Frames

You Need:

- red, purple, pink, and white fun foam
- instant camera
- scissors
- magnetic tape
- black felt-tip pen
- glue

Before the Party:

- Use the pattern on page 116 and cut a frame for each student from purple fun foam.
- Cut red, pink, and white fun foam into 3" squares.
- Cut magnetic tape into 2" strips.

1. Cut hearts from the foam squares and glue them around the frame leaving the bottom edge blank.

2. Write "Hug Me" on the blank edge of the frame.

3. Take a photograph of each student.

4. Glue the picture on the back of their frame.

5. Place a magnetic strip on the back of the picture.

You Need:

- red poster board
- markers
- glue
- variety of candy

Candy Grams

Before the Party:

- Cut out one large heart for each child from the poster board.

1. Write a note to someone special substituting actual candy for words.
Suggested notes:

> I would travel to <u>Mars</u> to find parents like you!
> I'm a <u>sucker</u> for your love.
> You are a <u>sweetheart</u>!
> You bring me <u>mounds</u> of joy!
> You are my little <u>bit of honey</u>!

2. Sign the card: <u>Hugs and kisses,</u>
(student's name)

Bouquets of Love

Before the Party:
- Cut tissue paper into 5" squares.

1. Place 4 sheets of tissue one on top of another. Accordion fold the tissue in 1/2″ pleats.

2. Wrap one end of a pipe cleaner tightly around the center of the tissue folds.

3. Separate each tissue fold to form a flower.

4. Group 3 or 4 flowers together to make a bouquet.

5. When the students get home, they can put the bouquet of flowers in a vase.

Blooming Bookmarks

Before the Party:
- Press the flowers for several days or use store bought dried flowers.
- Cut white tag board into 3" x 9" strips.
- Cut contact paper into 5" x 10" pieces.

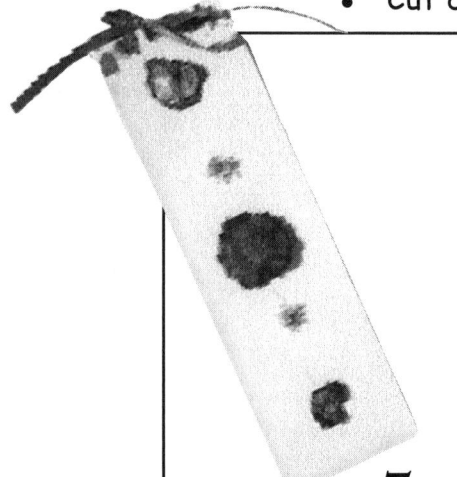

1. If this bookmark is for a gift, write a message on the back side of the tag board.

2. Glue flowers onto the front of the tag board.

3. Remove the paper covering on the contact paper and lay it flat, sticky side up.

4. Place the bookmark face down onto the sticky side of the contact paper.

5. Press the contact paper edges around the back of the bookmark.

6. Punch a hole at the top and tie a ribbon through the hole.

From the Heart Coupons

You Need:
- 9" x 12" red fun foam
- thin, red curling ribbon
- pink, red, white, and purple copy paper
- paper punch
- valentine stickers

Before the Party:

For each child.....
- Cut 2, 4" hearts out of fun foam.
- Cut 6 - 8 , 4" hearts from the copy paper.
- Cut ribbon into 10" lengths.

1. On the paper hearts, write activities that can be done for the recipient of the book.
Suggested activities: *This coupon is good for...*

one hug
taking out the garbage
one back rub
washing the dishes
ten kisses

2. Write the name of the person receiving the coupon book on a fun foam heart to make a cover.

3. Punch 2 holes at the top of the hearts, thread a ribbon through the holes, and tie.

Sweetheart Frames

You Need:
- acrylic picture frames
- candy conversation hearts
- instant camera
- glue

1. Glue candy hearts on the outside edges of the frame. Let dry.

2. Take a photograph to be sent home in the frame.

Valentine Treats

For ease and neatness we suggest students prepare their party treats on paper plates.

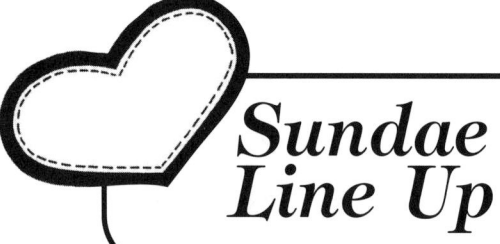

Sundae Line Up

You Need:
- new 10ft rain gutters
- ice cream scoop
- assorted ice cream toppings
- vanilla ice cream
- spoons
- napkins

Before the Party:
- Wash the gutters.

1. Students line up on both sides of the gutters.

2. Scoop ice cream for each student.

3. Pass the toppings down the line for students to take what they want.

4. Line up each new group of students at a clean section of the gutter.

You Need:
- refrigerated pizza dough
- mozzarella cheese
- toaster oven or oven
- heart-shaped cookie cutters
- pizza sauce
- pepperoni slices/pizza toppings
- pizza sauce
- spoons
- knives

Pizza You'll Love

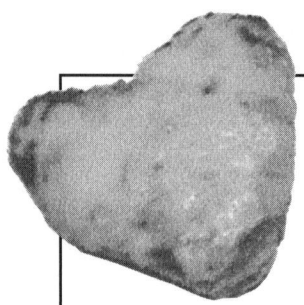

1. Students flatten a piece of pizza dough, then use the cookie cutter to cut a heart shape.

2. Spread the dough with pizza sauce and add pizza toppings. Cover with cheese.

3. Bake in a toaster oven according to the package directions.

Tooty Fruity Treats

You Need:
- strawberries
- grapes
- maraschino cherries
- strawberry yogurt
- bananas
- melon pieces
- spoons
- bowls

<u>Before the Party:</u>
- Cut the fruit into bite size pieces.

1. Make a kabob by putting fruit pieces on a skewer.

2. Spoon yogurt into a bowl.

3. Dip the kabob in the yogurt to eat.

You Need:
- mini bagels
- plastic knives
- strawberry cream cheese

Berry Good Bagels

1. Spread the cream cheese on the mini bagels.

Fruity Pizza

You Need:
- large sugar cookies
- pink frosting
- bite sized pieces of fruit such as kiwi, strawberries, mandarin oranges, peaches, blueberries

1. Students spread frosting on top of the cookie and add fruit.

Sweet Strawberries

You Need:
- large strawberries
- white chocolate
- bamboo skewers
- microwave, fondue pot, or crock pot
- chocolate
- waxed paper

<u>Before the Party:</u>
- Melt the chocolate.

1. Pierce a strawberry with a skewer and dip the strawberry into the chocolate.

2. Place on waxed paper to harden.
(It will harden quickly and be ready to eat.)

You Need:
- red and pink candy coated chocolate pieces
- donut-shaped sweetened cereal
- peanuts
- raisins
- sunflower nuts
- spoons
- large valentine paper cups
- red gumdrops
- candy hearts
- dried fruit
- bowls

Take N' Shake

<u>Before the Party:</u>
- Place food items in individual bowls.

1. Scoop the desired food items to fill a cup half full.

2. Place a hand tightly over the top of the cup and shake up the snack.

Licorice Leis

You Need:
- shoestring red licorice
- assorted donut-shaped cereal
- yogurt pretzels
- gummi rings
- hard candy rings

1. Thread the candy ring to the center of the licorice.

2. Thread cereal, pretzels and candy next to both sides of the ring and finish the necklace.

Pretty Pretzels

You Need:
- pretzel twists
- plastic knives
- chocolate covered candy pieces
- red and pink sprinkles
- red and pink frosting

1. Spread frosting on a pretzel and decorate it with candy and sprinkles.

You Need:
- bread
- knives
- mayonnaise
- heart-shaped cookie cutter
- variety of deli meat and cheese
- butter
- pickles
- mustard

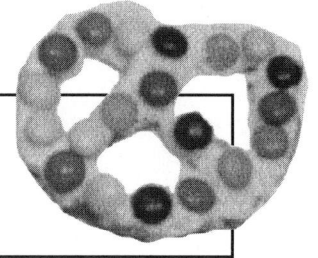

"Heart"y Sandwiches

1. Using the cookie cutter, cut hearts from two slices of bread.

2. Students make sandwiches of their choosing.

Love Bugs

You Need:
- 6 mini muffins
- frosting
- red shoestring licorice

1. With frosting, glue the mini muffins into a caterpillar shape.

2. Add licorice to the first muffin to make antennae.

Cookie Pops

You Need:
- refrigerated sugar cookie dough
- pink or red frosting
- craft sticks
- hot cinnamon candies
- candy sprinkles
- aluminum foil

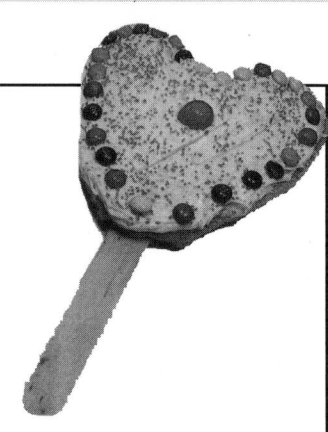

1. Give each student a slice of dough.

2. Using their hands, students flatten the dough 1/2" thick and form a heart.

3. Carefully insert a craft stick in the base of the cookie dough heart.

4. Follow the baking instructions on the package.

5. Decorate the cookie pops when cooled.

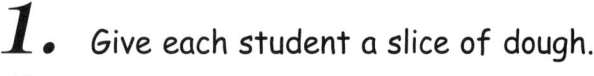

Strawberry Floats

You Need:
- vanilla ice cream
- strawberry soda
- fresh strawberries
- large cups
- spoons
- straws

1. Scoop ice cream into the cups.

2. Pour soda over the ice cream.

3. Top with a strawberry.

4. Serve with a straw and spoon.

Honey Bear Biscuits

1. Give each student a piece of foil.

2. Place one biscuit on the foil.

3. Divide the other biscuit in half.

4. Press the halves to the top of the whole biscuit to form ears.

5. Bake according to package directions.

6. Spread with honey and make a bear's face using raisins, peanut butter and chocolate chips.

Names to Nibble

1. Spread pink frosting on a whole graham cracker.

2. Using white frosting, students write their first names.

3. Decorate using sugar sprinkles.

Cupid's Arrows

You Need:
- chocolate covered cake rolls
- wooden skewers
- 4" red pipe cleaner pieces (2 per child)
- large red gummi hearts

1. Twist two pipe cleaners to the base of the skewer to form the arrow's feathers.

2. Push the skewer through the cake roll.

3. Place a gummi heart at the point of the arrow.

Hearts a Flutter

You Need:
- 5" celery pieces
- soft cream cheese
- 2" red shoestring licorice pieces (2 per child)
- pretzel twists
- red sprinkles

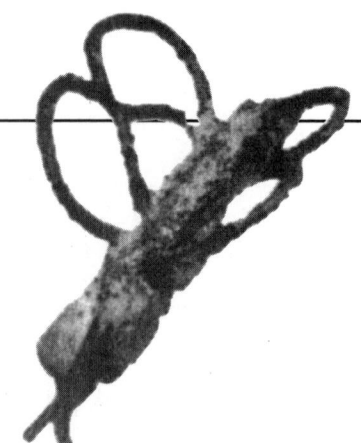

1. Spread cream cheese onto celery.

2. Cover with red sprinkles.

3. Place two pretzels in the cream cheese to form wings.

4. Add licorice to make antennae.

Reproducible Pages

Opposites Attract *from page 9*

up	down	hot	cold	happy
sad	white	black	fast	slow
girl	boy	rich	poor	good
bad	friend	enemy	love	hate
start	finish	weak	strong	walk
run	sit	stand	clean	dirty

Funny Bones from page 11

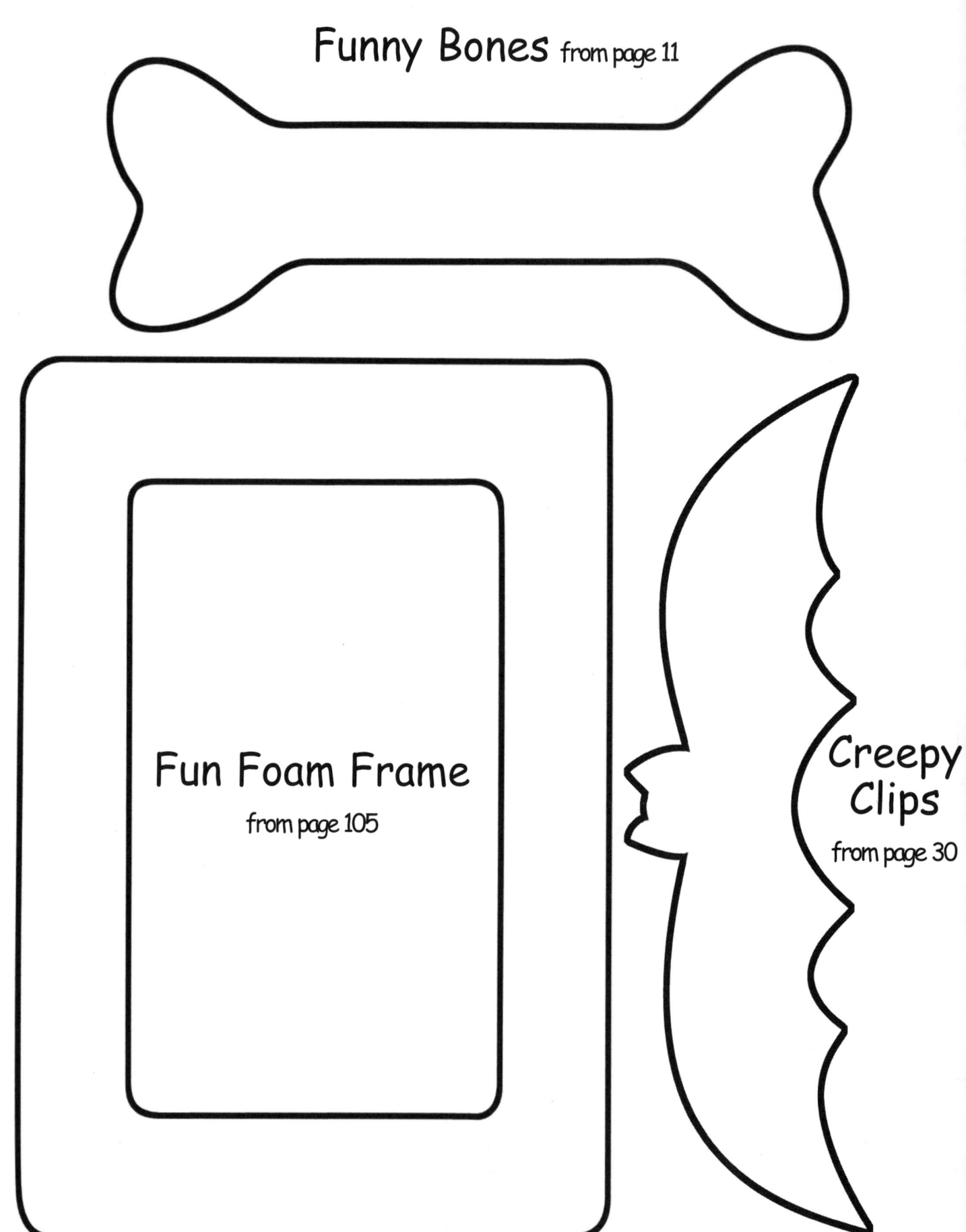

Fun Foam Frame

from page 105

Creepy Clips

from page 30

Pumpkin Peekers *from page 32*

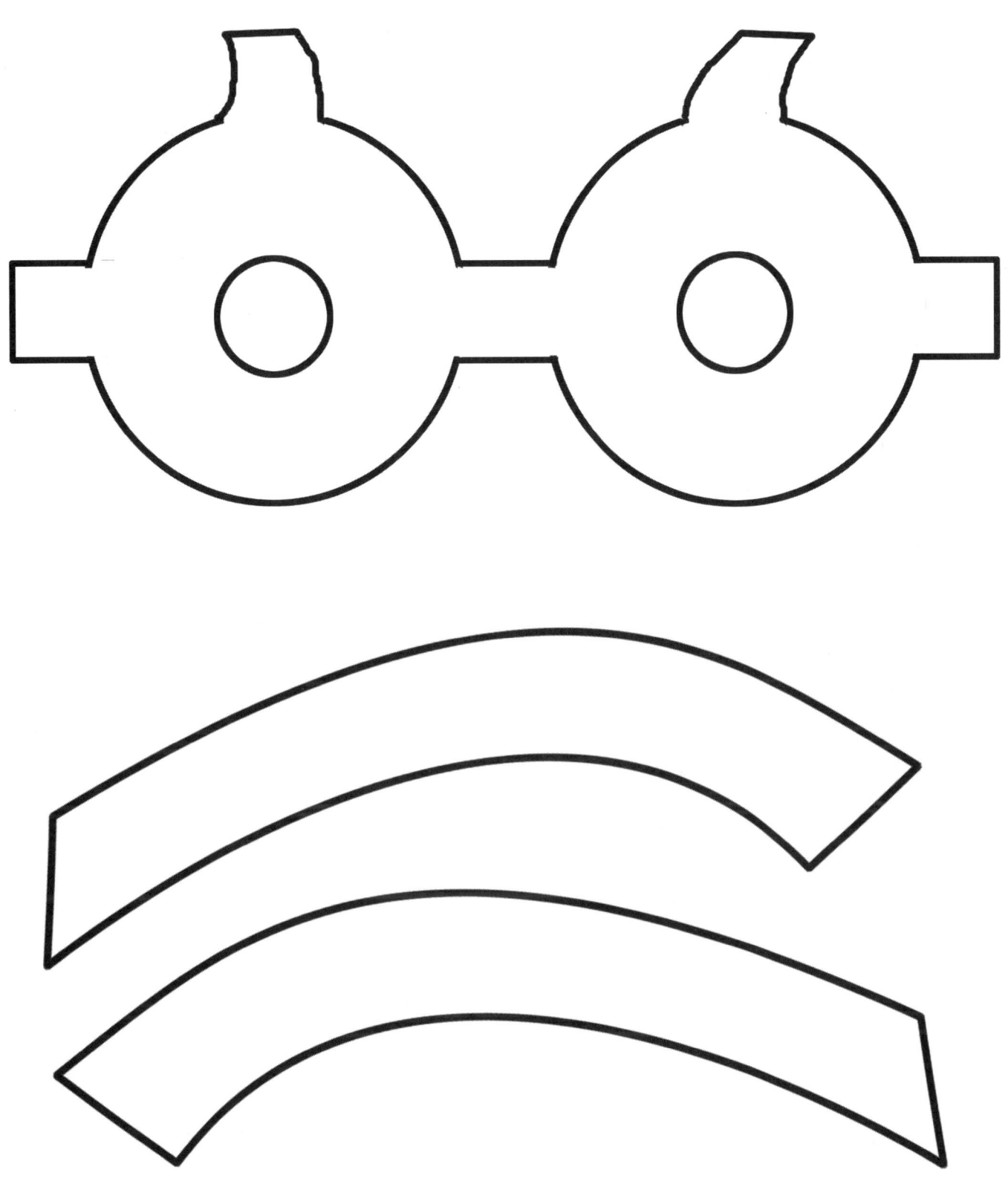

Reproducible – *Parties With Pizzazz*

Spooky Settings from page 35   # Bat The Bat from page 23

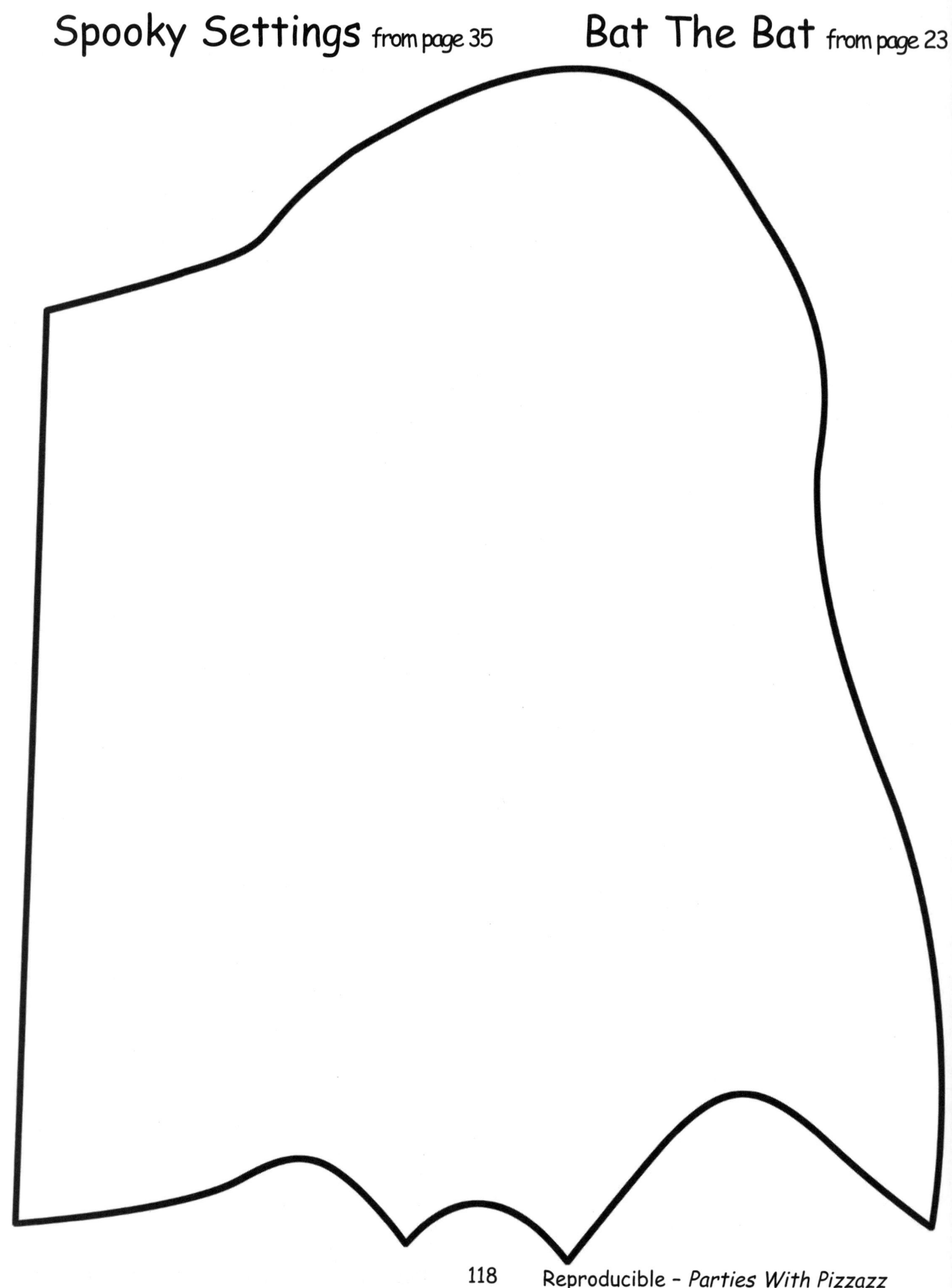

Reproducible – *Parties With Pizzazz*

Blizzard Buddies *from page 47*

	Do you like winter?	
	Is your birthday in December?	
	Are your socks white?	
Do you like pizza?	Do you have a snowboard?	Do you like to skate?
Do you have a cat?	Have you ever gone skiing?	Are you wearing green?
Do you have a brother?	Do you like math?	Is blue your favorite color?
	Is your winter hat blue?	
	Do you like hot chocolate?	
	Do you have brown eyes?	

Reproducible – *Parties With Pizzazz*

The Same Game from page 49

big	large	easy	simple	fast
quick	frown	scowl	munch	nibble
happy	jolly	mad	angry	loud
noisy	odd	weird	afraid	scared
sick	ill	throw	toss	small
tiny	yell	shout	jump	leap

Snowman Shake *from page 53*

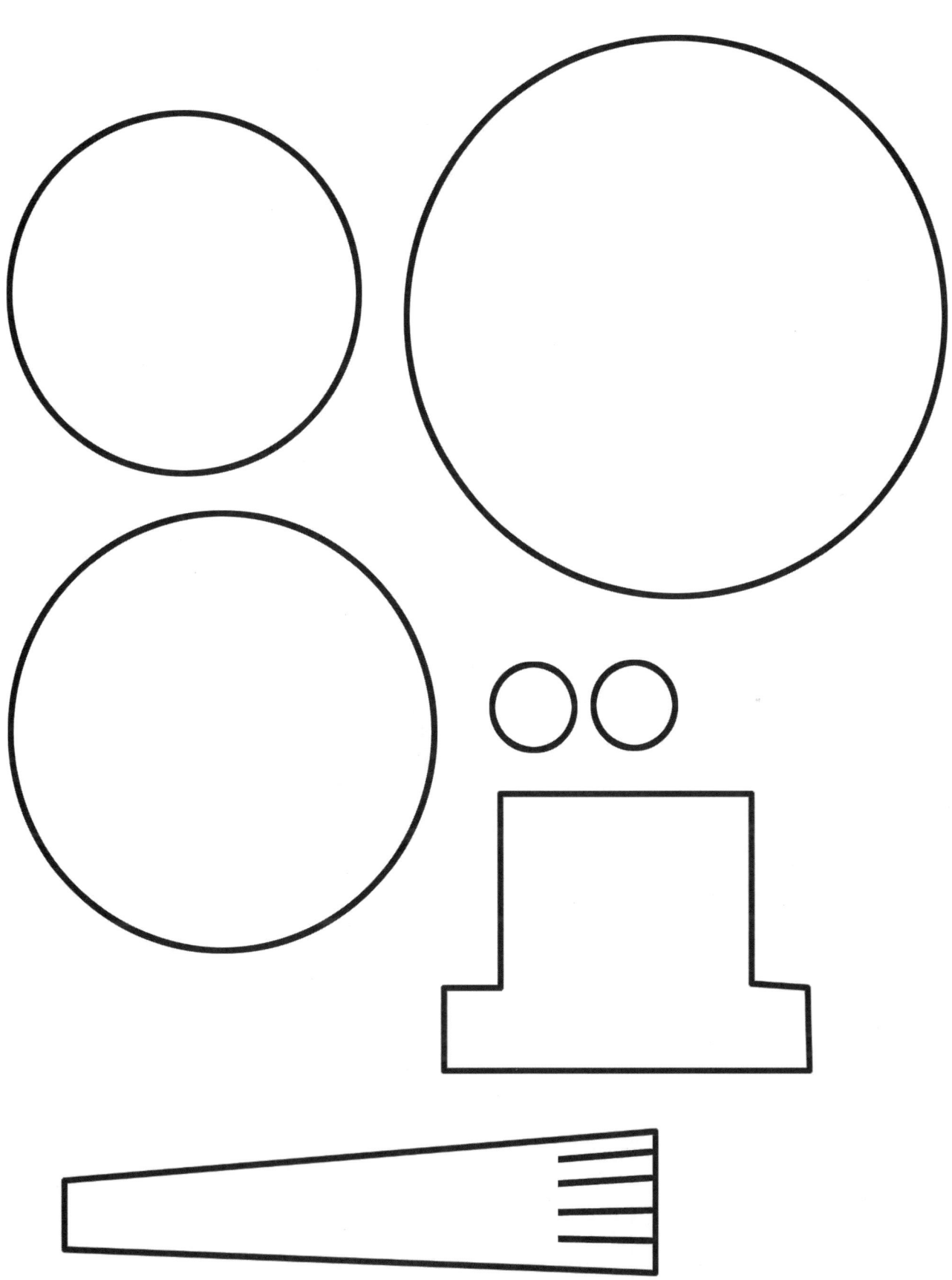

Reproducible – *Parties With Pizzazz*

Blizzard Bowling *from page 59*

Name _____   <u>Scorecard</u> - Each pin equals one point.

1	2	3	4	5	6	7	8	9

Name _____   <u>Scorecard</u> - Each pin equals one point.

1	2	3	4	5	6	7	8	9

Picture Perfect Snowmen *from page 68*

Snowboard Race

from page 57

Stitched Stockings *from page 71*

Magazine Maze from page 89

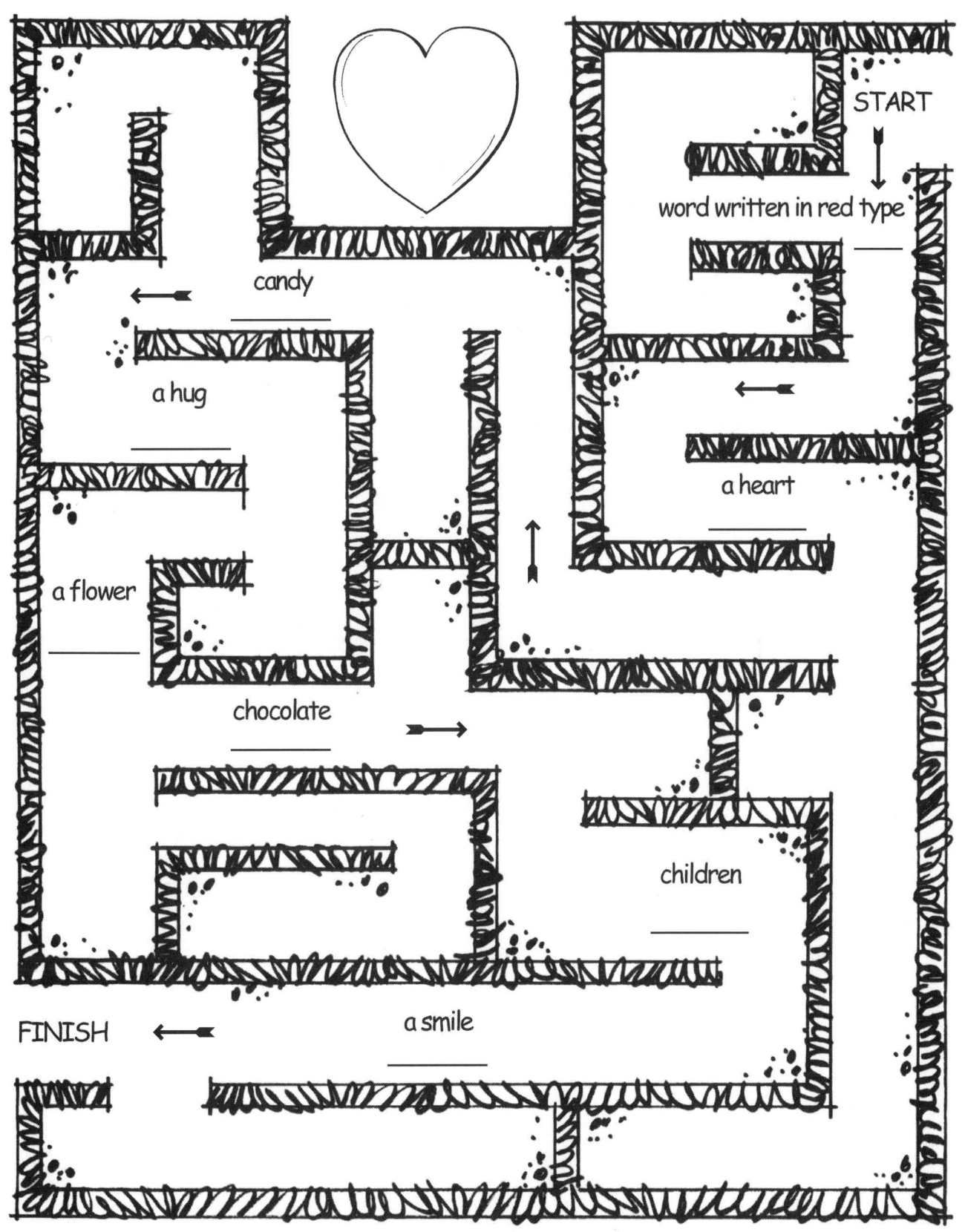

START

word written in red type ___

a heart ___

children ___

candy

a hug ___

a flower ___

chocolate ___

a smile ___

FINISH

On a Roll from page 96

Reproducible – *Parties With Pizzazz*

Keepsake Quotes

Love from, _____

1. Better to be safe than _____.

2. It's always darkest before_____.

3. Never underestimate the power of_____.

4. You can lead a horse to water but_____

    _____.

5. Don't bite the hand that _____.

6. No news is _____.

7. You can't teach an old dog _____.

8. Love all, trust _____.

9. The pen is mightier than _____.

10. Where there's smoke, there's _____

    _____.

11. A penny saved is a_____.

12. Two is company, three's _____.

13. If at first you don't succeed, _____

    _____.

14. You get out of something what you_____

    _____.

15. Laugh and the whole world laughs with you.
    Cry and_____.

Order Your Copy Of
Parties with
PiZZAZZ

A Complete Resource for Holiday Parties

Pizzazz Publishing
(952) 368-1903

www.pizzazzpublishing.com

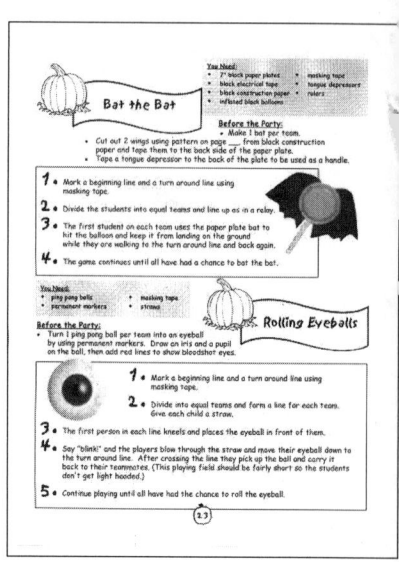

Yes! Send . . .	QUANTITY	PRICE	TOTAL
Parties with PiZZAZZ	_____	$19.95 ea.	$_____
SHIPPING & HANDLING		$ 4.00 ea.	$_____
		TOTAL:	$_____

Name: _____   Name: _____

Address: _____   Address: _____

City: _____ State: _____   City: _____ State: _____

Zip: _____ Phone: (____) _____   Zip: _____ Phone: (____) _____

☐ Check or Money Order payable to: **Pizzazz Publishing**

☐ Credit Card: _____ Visa _____ Master Card _____ Discover

Card Number: _____ Expiration date: _____

Name on Card: _____

Signature: _____

Mail your payment and order form to: Pizzazz Publishing
P.O. Box 415
Victoria, Minnesota 55386

Party Planners

Teachers

Librarians

128   Reproducible – *Parties With Pizzazz*